Trapped Giant:
China's Military Rise

Jonathan Holslag

Trapped Giant:
China's Military Rise

Jonathan Holslag

IISS The International Institute for Strategic Studies

The International Institute for Strategic Studies

Arundel House | 13–15 Arundel Street | Temple Place | London | WC2R 3DX | UK

First published November 2010 by **Routledge**
4 Park Square, Milton Park, Abingdon, Oxon, OX14 4RN

for **The International Institute for Strategic Studies**
Arundel House, 13–15 Arundel Street, Temple Place, London, WC2R 3DX, UK
www.iiss.org

Simultaneously published in the USA and Canada by **Routledge**
270 Madison Ave., New York, NY 10016

Routledge is an imprint of Taylor & Francis, an Informa Business

DIRECTOR-GENERAL AND CHIEF EXECUTIVE John Chipman
EDITOR Nicholas Redman
ASSISTANT EDITOR Janis Lee
EDITORIAL Tim Huxley, Ayse Abdullah, Douglas Barrie, Henry Boyd, Gary Li,
Christian Le Miére
COVER/PRODUCTION John Buck
COVER IMAGES iStockphoto.com

The International Institute for Strategic Studies is an independent centre for research, information and debate on the problems of conflict, however caused, that have, or potentially have, an important military content. The Council and Staff of the Institute are international and its membership is drawn from almost 100 countries. The Institute is independent and it alone decides what activities to conduct. It owes no allegiance to any government, any group of governments or any political or other organisation. The IISS stresses rigorous research with a forward-looking policy orientation and places particular emphasis on bringing new perspectives to the strategic debate.

The Institute's publications are designed to meet the needs of a wider audience than its own membership and are available on subscription, by mail order and in good book-shops. Further details at www.iiss.org.

Printed and bound in Great Britain by Bell & Bain Ltd, Thornliebank, Glasgow

British Library Cataloguing in Publication Data
A catalogue record for this book is available from the British Library

Library of Congress Cataloging in Publication Data

ADELPHI series
ISSN 0567-932X

ADELPHI 416
ISBN 978-0-415-66989-4

Contents

January 2009: four smoke-grey F-22 *Raptors* taxi slowly down the runway of Andersen Air Force base, Guam, an island in the western Pacific that has been gradually transformed into a major US military bridgehead. From Andersen, it takes less than two hours for an F-22 to reach Japan, Taiwan, the strategic sea lanes of Southeast Asia or the restless South China Sea. The presence of these aircraft bears witness to Washington's changing strategic focus: at the same time as it has been reducing its military presence over the Atlantic, it has boosted its prowess in the Pacific. 'The reason is obvious,' a senior military adviser in Washington has said. 'We might still be preoccupied with terrorists and Iraq, but in the middle-long term there will be only one main concern for the United States armed forces, and that is China. China is reshaping the military order in Asia, and it is doing so at our expense.'[1] In the same vein, in September 2009 US Secretary of Defense Robert Gates explicitly warned that the People's Liberation Army (PLA) was stepping up its ability to disrupt America's 'freedom of movement' and to narrow its 'strategic options'.[2] Similar echoes have become increasingly audible in Canberra, New Delhi, Tokyo and even Moscow and Seoul.

So, to what extent has the People's Republic of China (PRC) been gaining military power in Asia and what are the consequences for regional security? To answer this, one must consider many variables such as military capabilities, geopolitical characteristics, perceptions and evolving security identities, beyond the US-centric approach that has characterised much of the recent research on the topic. Hitherto, the discussion about China's growing military prowess has developed essentially around the question of how the Asian juggernaut tests Washington's resolve and capacity as the dominant power in the Pacific.[3] Since the Second World War, the United States has maintained preponderance in the region by means of unequalled forward military presence and an extensive web of security alliances. After the demise of the Soviet Union, China is emerging as the second power that might alter the military balance in a way that fundamentally reshapes the regional security order. It is unlikely that the future military balance in Asia will be purely bipolar; the region's security will depend as much on the emerging multipolar substructure as the new bipolar superstructure. China has gained military power vis-à-vis the US mainly by deploying asymmetric deterrence to weaken the latter's maritime supremacy, but these potential gains in security could be offset by new arms races with regional protagonists such as India and Japan.

While global challenges such as terrorism, financial instability and climate change continue to occupy policymakers, examining the military balance in Asia may look increasingly anachronistic. However, while leaders need to be prepared for a wide range of non-traditional threats, they need to be aware of the impact of old-fashioned military rivalry among nations. China's military modernisation is clearly one of the main factors that could destabilise the military balance and cause a chain reaction in Asia and beyond, prompting nations to revise policies to protect their security interests, by investing in costly defence systems, reshaping alliances and reassessing the consequences of traditional military power-plays for the prospect of international cooperation on non-traditional security threats.

Analysing the changing patterns of military contest will also be crucial to anticipating the future trajectory of great-power politics. Changes in countries' armed forces remain one of the most reliable indicators of how they perceive the international order. Political leaders and experts increasingly stress that international relations in the twenty-first century will be different from what has gone before. China insists that it will steer clear of the great-power rivalry trap and that its rise will be peaceful. In its 2002 position paper on the New Security Concept (*xin anquan guan*) the Chinese Ministry of Foreign Affairs said: 'Force cannot fundamentally resolve disputes and conflicts, and a security regime based on the use of force or the threat to use force can hardly bring about lasting peace.'[4] In a world that is characterised by intensifying interdependence (*xianghu yicun*), the paper pointed out, it was not necessary for China to achieve military primacy. Prominent scholars such as Zhang Yunling, Yang Yin and Wang Yizhou highlight China's growing reliance on foreign markets as a key reason for practising restraint and contributing to the regional and global common goods.[5] Yang Yi, director of the China Institute for International Strategic Studies (CIISS), observed: 'In order to avoid the kind of security dilemma in which many rising powers historically have been trapped, China must use its increasing economic power to promote prosperity and development in the region and the world.'[6] Even sceptics argue that peaceful development is the only option for China.[7] Pointing to the failure of overambitious land powers such as Nazi Germany and the Soviet Union, they maintain that restraint (*kezhi*) is vital if China is to avoid the devastating costs of war.[8]

China's military transition could, therefore, be the litmus test for such a paradigm shift.

Similarly, a study of the military relations between China and other regional protagonists could help to assess whether it will be possible to manage the altering balance of power by drawing China into a set of cooperative values. Since the late 1990s, the West has tried to steer China towards becoming a 'responsible' power. In 2005, then Deputy Secretary of State Robert Zoellick put it thus:

> It is time to take our policy beyond opening doors to China's membership into the international system. We need to urge China to become a responsible stakeholder in that system ... in doing so China could achieve to transcend the traditional ways for great powers to emerge.[9]

If Beijing is persuaded to take part in military cooperation, the fixation with traditional threats could be replaced with a new focus on non-traditional threats and a joint approach to shouldering the burden of maintaining stability. Testifying before the US Senate in 2009, Timothy Keating, then-Chief of the US Pacific Command (PACOM) said:

> We are cautiously optimistic ... we seek a mature and constructive relationship with our counterparts. Through cooperation we aim to reduce the chances of miscalculation, increase mutual understanding, and encourage cooperation in areas of common interest.[10]

As China becomes more integrated with the global market, it may realise that its interest is best served by collective policing of global commons instead of exclusive control over a limited sphere of influence. Since the late 1990s, the Pentagon has signalled that China should not think of establishing its own security perimeter, for instance by emphasising its freedom of navigation in the South China Sea. But at the same time it invited Beijing to take part in missions to tackle piracy in the Indian Ocean or hunt terrorists in Central Asia. A decade of such engagement, added to China's growing awareness of the security risks that attend its 'go-global' economic strategy, testify to Beijing's apparent change of attitude. If indeed a new kind of collective or multilateral military thinking emerges from this, it would significantly cut the risk of an arms race.[11] China's military transition should thus be considered a possible precursor of its development into a leading international actor and as a measure of the success of constructive engagement policies.

Measuring military power: parameters and actors

Military power is the ultimate instrument that disciplines politicians and diplomats. But how can we measure it? Recent studies of China's military power have produced different answers to the same question. On the one hand, experts have cautioned that China's armed forces are still poorly developed. Building on his authoritative study on the PLA, George Washington University's David Shambaugh said:

> What China has purchased, which attracted a lot of media attention, is not very great in numbers and not even state-of-the-art. The Chinese indigenous defence capability is really very poor, particularly in aircraft and submarines.[12]

This idea of the PLA still being a hollow force and the belief that it is only partially modernising has led various scholars to conclude that the military balance in Asia will not alter rapidly. Chinese security experts also used to play down the PLA's clout in comparison to US military might. On the other hand, it was argued that China has reduced the qualitative gap between the PLA and other armed forces. While not a military power with global scope, the PLA has gained recognition as a leading regional player with a growing international range. This discrepancy is mainly due to an inconsistent use of parameters. Some studies have been limited to counting cannons and missiles, and left out important qualitative variables like organisation and experience. Some used the United States' military capabilities as their benchmark, while others looked at Taiwan. Analyses also attached varying importance to indigenisation of military technology. Many recent assessments are also still founded on balances of power from the 1990s, when China was indeed struggling to operate various new arms systems it had bought in from Russia and was still building the first advanced, indigenously designed arms systems. Moreover, conservative estimates often did not consider the recent strains experienced by American forces in Asia as a consequence of the war on terror or by budgetary constraints. Hence, an update of the Sino-American military balance is overdue, and particular attention should be given to the quantitative and qualitative improvement of China's new military equipment and the extent to which this could have affected the dominance of the US forces in the Pacific.

Taiwan remains the focal point of China's force posturing, training and doctrine, in spite of the recent thaw in cross-straits relations. Military leaders said as recently as 2007: 'The modernisation of the Chinese armed forces aims to achieve the ability to defend national sovereignty, security and reunification of the country.'[13] Various White Papers on National Defence also envisage Taiwanese secession as the ultimate threat to sovereignty.

The 2008 version, for example, confirmed the rapprochement at the political level, but still warned of 'separatist forces' and of the United States' ongoing arms sales to Taiwan, which it said caused 'serious harm to Sino-US relations as well as peace and stability across the Taiwan Straits'.[14] Statements like these reveal that the military balance with Taiwan cannot be separated from the military balance with the US. America's military hegemony in China's periphery continues to cause distrust, and its willingness to use its military power to protect US interests abroad is considered an important source of insecurity.[15] Wang Jisi of Peking University said:

> After the Cold War, the US continued to consolidate its military arrangements in the Asia Pacific of which a considerable part is directed against China. China and the US might not have become global opponents; [but] it is increasingly clear that they are regional opponents.[16]

Chinese observers have pointed to America's forward military presence in Asia as evidence of a new containment strategy.[17] But it also watches the other regional powers. Beijing's perception of Asia's strategic outlook is that of one superpower and multiple regional powers.[18] The latter are significant not only because some of them have a history of military competition with China, but also because of their role in the formation of military alliances around the United States. Chief among these are Australia, India, Japan, Russia and South Korea.

We can speak of a military power shift, if the change of one country's capabilities is leading to an important redistribution at the level of the regional power structure. In the case of China, the question is whether its military modernisation will be substantial enough to transform the essentially US-centric, military unipolar order into a bipolar order, or whether it will contribute to the creation of a multipolar order. In this regard it is important to identify the structural position of Taiwan. As mentioned earlier, the military balance with Taiwan is a key concern in China's strategising, but it only has an indirect impact on the power structure, because Taiwan can only raise the costs for China of changing that structure; it cannot change the structure itself. It simply cannot match China's military expenditure. In 2001, the mainland's official defence budget was already three times larger than Taiwan's. By 2008 it was spending six times as much. For our purposes, it will be useful to consider Taiwan not as a factor that shapes, but as an actor that mediates the regional balance of power.

Another point that needs to be clarified is how complete the modernisation of military capabilities has to be for a power shift to take place. It is obvious indeed that the state with the most complete arsenal has more options to wage war. But military power is also about the ability to flexibly control escalation without risking mutual destruction by detonating nuclear bombs. Yet, countries seldom lead in all forms of warfare. America and China have completely different forms of force posturing in Asia. Evaluating military balances is, therefore, often a matter of comparing tanks with missiles, ships with aircraft, navies with armies, and so on. Most military powers are niche players and how such asymmetric strengths translate into strategic advantages is unclear. In addition, power shifts tend to be diffuse, creeping processes and the three main structures – unipolar, bipolar and multipolar – are often just *archetypes* that show what kind of transformation may be expected. It is thus more relevant to look for continuous, rather than discrete, changes in the variables and to see how countries are managing to address gaps in their capabilities.

Evaluating the power shift

Washington has modified its posture in the Pacific in response to the changing military balance in Asia; it continues to evaluate its plans to modernise its capabilities. Beijing, meanwhile, is making progress in putting its coastal and off-shore defence strategy into practice. A combination of symmetric and asymmetric efforts has been made to undermine US hegemony and project power further into the Pacific Ocean. This aggravates the security dilemma to such a degree that it becomes increasingly difficult to imagine what the eventual status quo may look like. Interest in a continental-versus-maritime-power status quo will be offset by a security dilemma that encourages both powers to extend their defensive perimeter further into the Pacific Ocean. America's first line of defence starts in the Taiwan Strait, whereas China, fearful of containment, will continue to try to extend its military frontier closer to US shores. Such military strategies could turn the quest for security in the Pacific into a perilous zero-sum game and reduce the prospect for peaceful cooperation with regard to non-traditional threats.

But into this mix we must add the other regional powers. The military contest between China and the US has increased uncertainty among other Asian states.[19] While China develops the military means to protect its littoral periphery, its neighbours assume that this decreases their own security without being certain that the US will continue to be able to keep the giant's power in check. This can be observed from the recognition of China's military strength, the fixation with the proximity of China's military presence to borders or vital sea lanes, uncertainty about whether China's development will continue to be peaceful, and finally the fear of new offensive capabilities, or the inability to distinguish between offensive and defensive systems, that can be used further afield than Taiwan. These growing concerns will in turn affect regional security. In spite of their common concern, an assessment of recent defence treaties, patterns of joint training, and arms trade reveals that collective counterbalancing has not occurred because of different threat calculations and ambitions. As these diverging postures coincide with rapidly but selectively increasing military capabilities, the bipolar super-structure of Asia's strategic landscape will become embedded in an emerging multipolar sub-structure that will be uncontrollable by either of the two main protagonists.

How will this affect the region's long-term security? Although it has apparently become more assertive in its military posturing since 2008, China's military modernisation is not yet perceived as an imminent threat. While most Asian countries see that they need to increase investment in their own militaries, they do not feel an urgent need to signal their ultimate intention by concluding formal defence pacts. This reluctance coincides with the cost-benefit calculus that forming alliances too soon might force China to expedite its military build-up, which would completely undermine regional stability and the prospects for prosperity through increased intra-Asian trade. All Asian powers have now identified the status of their countries, to a large degree, with success in tapping into international trade flows. They have ambitions to become trading states and prefer to thrive peacefully on the global market. But the political elites in countries such as India, Japan and Russia, are still torn between this new brand of constructive nationalism and the desire to create their own spheres of influence, or to gain prestige by means of military potency. This ambivalence has complicated the formation of new alliances, because if Asian powers again seek to become warrior states instead of networking states, the multi-polar Asian security system will be prone to fierce rivalry and armed conflict. Trade ambitions are likely to have a negative impact on military stability. The outcome of these security dilemmas centred around China's military modernisation is a strategic landscape that will be dominated not just by the interplay between America and China, but by the interaction between China and its neighbours, and by synergies between these other regional powers. Arms races could still be plausible scenarios for the new nucleus of global order.[20]

CHAPTER ONE

China's Rise and the Use of Force: A Historical and Geopolitical Perspective

Beijing's map

China is the geopolitical centre of Asia. This brings both the unequalled opportunity to wield region-wide influence and the challenge to handle other powers' ever-fluctuating spheres of influence. China perceives its security environment in three layers that can be summarised as the heartland, the frontier land and the belt of uncertainty, as illustrated in the map overleaf.

With about 90% of the Chinese population, 75% of the domestic production and all the major centres of political and economic power, the *heartland*, covering the first and second tier of coastal provinces, contains China's main interests. It is here that agriculture took root, great cultures bloomed and political power matured. The stability and prosperity of the heartland has been the main concern of the Chinese leadership since Mao Tsedong. The Chinese heartland is both continental and maritime.

The *frontier land* includes most of the territory that Beijing actually controls, as well as Taiwan, Arunachal Pradesh, most of the South China Sea, the East China Sea and the Yellow Sea.

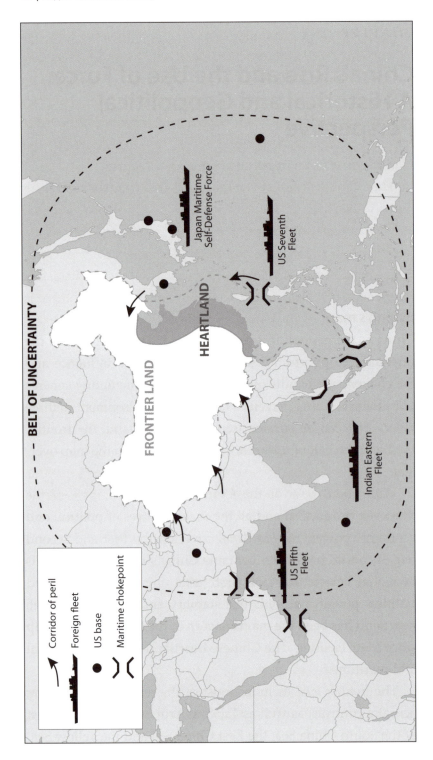

It is vital for its natural resources like oil, minerals, water and fish, and for access to other economically important areas in Asia and beyond. Historically, it also proved to be a stepping stone for other powers to threaten or invade the heartland, and was often an incubator and sanctuary of rebellion. Ethnic-minority groups in the periphery used to be considered by the Han majority as an important source of insecurity.

The stability and sovereignty of the frontier land is a precondition for the development of the heartland and the control of four main 'corridors of peril'. In the west, there is the Islamist trail, which forms the interface between the Uighurs in Xingjian and restless neighbouring countries such as Pakistan, Afghanistan, Tajikistan and Kyrgyzstan. In the south there is the Tibetan plain, which connects the Autonomous Region of Tibet with sanctuaries of Tibetan refugees in India, Nepal and Bhutan. Further west we find the narco nexus with the opium-producing Golden Triangle. Via ethnic-minority groups that live on both sides of the border, organised crime and violence spill over into China. Finally, there is the maritime corridor in the east: the main transit zone for colonial powers to start their conquest. Many Chinese still believe that the heartland is in danger as long as it – including Taiwan – is not effectively controlled. This all explains why Beijing is so alert to problems in the frontier land, and not least to territorial disputes and alleged interference by other powers.

Beyond the frontier land stretches a long belt of uncertainty. It includes most neighbouring countries. On the one hand, this zone harbours plenty of economic opportunities, ranging from raw materials to high-tech industry, which makes it a key target for economic cooperation. But China also approaches it with a strong sense of geopolitical claustrophobia. Various non-traditional security threats are looming in the Chinese neighbourhood: terrorism, piracy, illegal migration, organised

crime and environmental hazards. Traditional security dilemmas persist as other powers try to expand their influence. The
United States casts a long shadow with its military presence
from the Korean Peninsula all the way to Kyrgyzstan. Australia,
Japan, the Republic of Korea, Russia and Vietnam, are important secondary balancers, which could respond to China's rise
by forming alliances – either with each other or with the United
States. Tertiary balancers do not have the capacity to challenge
China. This league of intermediate states, however, has a habit
of playing China off against other powers and of diversifying
their military relations in response to China's growing clout.
The ambivalence of these states prompts Beijing to combine
confidence building with preventive counter-containment and
balancing strategies.

The PRC has a long history of using military force to maintain domestic stability, to guard its territorial integrity and to
obstruct interference from great powers into its immediate
neighbourhood. China's changing attitude to the use of force
has affected stability in Asia in important ways. Many Chinese
scholars of security affairs argue that their country has made
the most important contribution to stability in Asia by preserv-
ing the security of about a third of the Asian population during
the last four decades. After more than a century of humiliation
(1839–1949), civil war (1927–1950) and another nine years of
Cultural Revolution (1966–1975), economic growth and political effectiveness have paved the way for a new golden age, or
at least a period of strategic opportunity.[1] But military power
too continued to be an indispensible tool to repress looming
civil unrest. After the 1959 agreement that authorised Chinese
administration in Tibet (the 17-point Agreement for the Peaceful
Liberation of Tibet), troops were deployed in several peripheral
provinces to keep a close eye on ethnic minorities. Throughout
the 1980s and 1990s, the government frequently launched

strike-hard campaigns (*yan da*) to crack down on alleged seces-sionist movements and criminal gangs. To date, more than 100,000 PLA troops have been dispatched in the Autonomous Regions of Tibet and Xinjiang.[2] In 1982, Beijing also established the paramilitary People's Armed Police – which now counts almost 1.5 million officers – to control social unrest.

Despite China's fixation with sovereignty and a large number of territorial disputes, the use of force in such conflicts has been limited. As Taylor Fravel showed in his 2008 book *Strong Borders, Secure Nations*, internal challenges have often prompted China to compromise in its border conflicts with states.[3] It seems leaders calculated that cooperative relations with neighbouring countries were more important than gaining a few square kilometres of land. There were three notable exceptions to this, however: border conflicts with regional great powers, disputes over maritime demarcations and Taiwan. In 1962, China carried out an expedition in northern India to sanc-tion Delhi for an alleged intrusion in Tibet. In 1969, Chinese elite troops ambushed Soviet border guards on the disputed Zhenbao island in the Ussuri River. In contrast to the border conflicts it has had with many smaller states, these two cases involved major powers. Beijing certainly calculated that if it did not stand firm, India and the Soviet Union could intrude further into sensitive regions such as Tibet and Xinjiang. At the same time, Mao Tsedong was experiencing growing pressure at home to demonstrate political leadership. Both operations were carefully planned and limited in scope to prevent escala-tion.

China also resorted to the calibrated use of force in pressing its claims over disputed areas in the East and South China Sea. In 1988, the Chinese and Vietnamese navies clashed near the Spratly Islands, killing 65 Vietnamese sailors. In 1995, it occu-pied the Philippine-claimed Mischief Reef and a year later PLA

Navy (PLAN) vessels engaged in a gun battle with a Philippine navy ship. The Chinese military boosted its presence on several islands in the South China Sea in the 1990s and started patrolling more frequently in contested areas. But Taiwan has been and remains China's most sensitive territorial dispute.

The third and most recent occasion that tensions over the island threatened to boil over was in 1995–96, when the PRC carried out a series of missile tests over the Strait and conducted an amphibious assault exercise. This followed an apparent policy u-turn, in which Washington granted a visa to Taiwan's President Lee Teng-hui to deliver a speech on democratisation at Cornell University. The PRC suspected Lee of secessionist sympathies. At the height of the crisis, the US sent two aircraft carrier battle groups to the Straits to counter an expected invasion. Since this incident, Beijing has consistently demonstrated its resolve by building up its military might and staging offensive exercises alongside the Taiwan Strait. Here, however, as elsewhere, the government has learned from the US response to the crisis and has been cautious not to let tensions spiral out of control. Its naval relations, policy and strategy have been profoundly influenced by its experience in the Taiwan Straits.

Dramatic troop deployments have occurred across China's frontiers. In 1950, Mao dispatched about 270,000 People's Volunteer Army troops to Korea, in an attempt to stop the northward offensive of the allied forces. In 1979, Deng Xiaoping ordered 200,000 soldiers to cross the border with Vietnam to retaliate for the Vietnamese invasion in Cambodia. While the Korean War lasted three years, compared to a campaign of three weeks in Vietnam, both interventions were triggered by fears that imperial powers had become too dominant in China's immediate neighbourhood. Mao felt that if the allied forces gained control over the Korean Peninsula, it might become a dagger in China's heart. In a telegram to Josef Stalin on 2 October 1950, he warned: 'If we allow the United States to occupy all of Korea, Korean revolutionary power will suffer a fundamental defeat, and the American invaders will run more rampant, and have negative effects for the entire Far East.' In the same way, Beijing suspected that the Soviet–Vietnamese alliance could allow Moscow to trap China in a pincer strategy. Geopolitical claustrophobia – the fear of hostile great powers controlling neighbouring countries and possibly encircling China – has thus been a third important motivation for using force. It led Beijing to complement its territorial borders with strategic frontiers within which it would commit military force 'in pursuit of goals that it defines to be in its national interest'.[4] These more flexible security perimeters also prompted China to develop an active defence strategy to deter imperial powers from building bridgeheads in its vicinity.

But even this active defence strategy was a response to the posturing of the two superpowers, rather than an attempt to establish long-term dominance over neighbouring countries.[5] Apart from its intervention in Korea, China's use of force has never had a *decisive* impact on stability in Asia. At best it adjusted the balance of power between America and the Soviet Union. Even when violence spiralled out of control – for example, during the expeditions in Korea, India and Vietnam – Beijing in the end opted for restraint and pulled back. The question remains, however: what lies behind this prudent use of force? Was it China's strategic culture? Had China low confidence in its capabilities, or did it have other security priorities?

Every decision-maker works within a distinctive strategic culture, which can be best defined as a set of general beliefs and expectations that form the perceptual lens for evaluating the security environment.[6] Most studies of China's strategic culture have found that it is strongly rooted in political realism. Harvard's Alastair Ian Johnston, for example, concluded that

Chinese decision-makers tend to assume that conflict is a constant feature of human affairs, due to the threatening nature of adversaries in a zero-sum context. 'Accommodationist strategies or strictly defensive ones are generally not conceived as the best routes to state security,' Johnston observed.[7] 'Security [for China] is a product of superior military preparations'. Andrew Scobell argued that in the twenty-first century, Chinese leaders will probably continue to view the world in realpolitik terms, building up their fighting forces while downplaying their willingness to use them. 'Paradoxically,' Scobell wrote, 'the cult of defence produces a Beijing ready to employ military force assertively against perceived external or internal threats, all while insisting that China possesses a cultural aversion to using force, doing so only defensively and solely at last resort.'[8] Research into Chinese policy documents and statements by the senior leadership has revealed enduring distrust of the hegemonic intentions of other powers and the awareness that ambitious powers could still invoke instability in other countries as a pretext for intervention. As Michael Pillsbury writes: 'The Chinese assessment of the current and future security environment depicts the present world as being in an era of transition to a new world structure. During this period, great rivalries will emerge among the powers, and many local wars will be fought, as a re-division of spheres of influence and a struggle for world leadership takes place.'[9]

A strategic culture that mixes offensive and defensive realism alone cannot explain China's self-restraint in using military force; low self-confidence and specific security priorities also made an important difference. In spite of two decades of drastic restructuring and modernisation, the Chinese leadership has not been fully confident that its armed forces could win wars under high-tech conditions without having to sacrifice strategic interests such as economic development or the supply of natural resources. These precise domestic interests have figured more prominently in Beijing's recent agenda than the need to keep other powers out of its backyard. As Wang Jisi puts it:

> Since the early 1980s, economic interests have grad-ually replaced strategic concerns in sustaining the expansion of China's international ties. The siege mentality is gone. Beijing's foreign policy principally serves to maximize China's economic interest and political integrity.[10]

This may be overstating the transformation in China's strategic calculus. Although it is certainly correct that economic objectives have gained the upper hand, there is evidence that the siege mentality is still a feature of China's strategic thinking. What may be better described as a recalibration was evident in Foreign Minister Tang Jiaxuan's address to the UN General Assembly in 2004:

> The first ten to twenty years of this century present China [with] an important strategic window of opportunity for its development. While taking development as our number one priority, we must grasp the opportunities, deepen reform, open the country still wider to the outside world, promote development and maintain stability.[11]

States always have a hierarchy of security priorities in which different threats are ranked according to needs and circumstances at a given moment. In China's case, these needs are centrally defined by the national political elite, but not without recognising the need to maintain the confidence of its people.

As with every nation, the attempt to gain legitimacy is a trade-off between efficiently meeting basic expectations such as stability and wealth on the one hand, and defending important values with which most compatriots identify themselves on the other. The hierarchy of priorities is thus not static, so strategic self-restraint cannot be taken for granted. The three most important variables that determine China's willingness to resort to force are, and will continue to be: the impact of the external environment on the legitimacy of the Chinese political elite, the cost of military force relative to the fulfilment of economic expectations and the conflict between interests and values in the strategic calculations of the Chinese government.

CHAPTER TWO

Engaging the Hegemon

Controlling the maritime margins of Asia

Since the nineteenth century, the US has considered the Pacific Ocean as both a conveyer belt to Asian markets and a buffer against emerging great powers on the Eurasian continent. As such, it needed to be controlled. Theodore Roosevelt said: 'Our interests are as great in the Pacific as in the Atlantic. Merely for the protection of our shores we need a great navy. And what is more we need it to protect our interests in the island from which it is possible to command our shores and to protect our commerce on the high seas.'[1] It was commerce that first lured the emerging superpower to the Philippines and the shores of China, but it was the deep-seated fear of losing this vital maritime space to other powers that has dominated Washington's strategising for more than a century since. In his seminal essay 'The Problem of Asia', Alfred Thayer Mahan cautioned that great navies based on coastal areas of Asia could, if not checked, threaten America's security.[2] A strong continental-based land power could defeat its neighbours, consolidate control over its maritime periphery and subsequently become a great sea power too.

Ever since, the US has followed a two-track strategy. On the one hand, it aimed to establish a maritime perimeter as close to the Asian continent as possible. In line with Mahan's thinking, US Secretary of State Dean Acheson proposed in the late 1940s to establish a security perimeter from Japan all the way to Australia, beyond which the Soviet Union should not be permitted to trespass.[3] George Kennan, then-Director of Policy Planning at the State Department, contended that the Soviet threat in East Asia was more about hostility than about capability, and that the US should, therefore, withdraw from the 'unsound commitments' on the East Asian continent and preserve Okinawa and the entire Ryukyu Islands group as an occupied fortress in East Asia for 'a long time to come'.[4] In 1950, General Douglas MacArthur said the American defence line in the Pacific 'runs through the chain of islands fringing the coast of Asia. It starts from the Philippines and continues through the Ryukyu archipelago, which includes its main bastion, Okinawa. Then it bends back through Japan and the Aleutian Island chain to Alaska.'[5] Not long after he made this expansive description, however, the Korean War forced the US back onshore, arousing the fear that the Russians would strengthen their presence in the east, and, as then-Secretary of State John Foster Dulles warned, that they would 'begin their objective of driving us out of the western Pacific, right back to Hawaii, and even to the United States'.[6] This prompted Washington again to concentrate on continental Asia and to try to prevent the communists from strengthening their grip over the region, first by containing them, later by pursuing a divide-and-rule policy between Moscow and Beijing.[7] The US's traditional security strategy can thus be summarised as ruling the Pacific waves and dividing the continent.

Washington's post-Cold War military superiority in East Asia still centres on the capacity to defend the continental

United States against an attack by one of the major powers in the region, as well as the ability to deter or dissuade Asian challengers from harming other vital American interests, by means of punitive strikes and denial operations.[8] This ambition has led it to sustain the US Pacific Command (PACOM) as the largest of its six regional commands. PACOM's force projection in the region rests on the permanent deployment of advanced platforms in the Pacific and Indian Oceans and the positioning of troops at various strategic forward locations. With an eye on China's military modernisation, the 2006 US *Quadrennial Defense Review* was firm in underlining the importance of 'forward-deployed forces and flexible deterrent options [to] dissuade any military competitor from developing disruptive or other capabilities that could enable regional hegemony or hostile action against the United States or other friendly countries'.[9] In the same vein, PACOM stated its aim 'to retain at least the current level of force presence and posture [and to] maintain military superiority across the full spectrum of operation'. China's military modernisation was invoked as a key justification to this end.[10]

US armed forces remain the most powerful in East Asia. The Navy operates a fleet of nuclear aircraft carriers, six of which are assigned to PACOM alone. One is permanently stationed in Japan. These vessels collectively carry up to 500 aircraft, including around 180 F/A-18 fighter jets (hereafter referred to as F-18s) and 120 of the more advanced F/A-18 E/F *Super Hornets*. This strike power has been further enhanced by 31 nuclear attack submarines, including the *Los Angeles* class and the more modern *Virginia* class, which each have 12 launch tubes for land-attack or anti-ship missiles. By the end of 2009, PACOM operated 12 guided-missile cruisers, 29 guided-missile destroyers and 12 frigates, which have a combined complement of 3,984 vertical launch tubes for *Tomahawk* cruise missiles,

Standard surface-to-air missiles or ASROC anti-submarine missiles.[11] This gives PACOM the capacity to carry out large onshore punitive strikes as well as sea denial operations, that is, blocking other countries' access to shipping routes and specific spheres of interest. Surface combatants were equipped with state-of-the-art air-defence capabilities. By 2008, the American fleet in the Pacific included destroyers and missile cruisers fitted with a new *Aegis* command and control system and SM-3 anti-ballistic missiles.[12]

To support this sea-based force, America has been modernising its network of facilities in the Pacific Rim. PACOM has built several new forward bases on Hawaii and Guam to add to the 34 permanent bases it maintains in the Republic of Korea (ROK) and Japan as of 2008. At the same time, the US has signed access agreements with seven other Asian countries. In spite of a series of programmes to reconsider America's foreign military presence, notably the Global Posture Review and the Base Realignment and Closure schemes, its footprint in East Asia was not much affected compared to the armed forces it stationed in Europe during that time. Between 2002 and 2008, 48,000 soldiers were withdrawn from Hawaii, Japan and the ROK, but in the same period, the number of troops in Guam increased by 3,300.[13] At the end of 2008, the US still had more than 120,000 soldiers deployed in the region.[14] All in all, the Pentagon's posture review in the Pacific has led to realignment rather than closure, and to modernisation instead of downscaling.

Guam, Hawaii and Japan have been consolidated as America's maritime strongholds in the Pacific. In recent years, Hawaii has been permanently modernised as the central node for operations in the Pacific. In 2004, the Joint Air Operations Centre at Hickam Air Force Base was modernised with the new Joint Fires Network (JFN), a technology that allows target information to be shared and distributed between forces.[15] In 2005, the Army Air Missile Defence Command was established, the first outside the continental US, to provide PACOM with robust theatre-based command and control.[16] In 2007, the Pentagon approved a new Intelligence Squadron Operations Facility for backing surveillance operations by the *Global Hawk* and *Predator* unmanned aerial vehicles (UAVs), and U-2 reconnaisance aircraft in the Asia-Pacific. In 2009, the US government started an $800 million programme to modernise the shipyard of Pearl Harbor, particularly so that new *Virginia*-class submarines could be stationed there. Two-thirds of the total fleet of *Virginia*-class submarines are to be based in Hawaii.[17] Likewise, Hickam was the first non-continental base to have its F-15 fighter jets replaced with 20 F-22 *Raptors*, and this operation has been accompanied by the refurbishment of maintenance and command infrastructure.

At a total cost of $15 billion, Guam has been turned into a joint-force inter-theatre hub and a stepping stone for long-range operations in Asia-Pacific.[18] According to Defense Secretary Robert Gates, the island is expected to serve as 'the nation's first line of defence and a robust military presence in a critical part of the world'.[19] In 2006, construction began on various new intelligence, surveillance and reconnaissance facilities at Andersen Air Force Base, with new shelters for *Global Hawk* UAVs, logistics for permanently deployed freighters and tankers, new infrastructure to support the long-term presence of fighters and facilities for an additional 24 rotationally deployed fighters, provisions for cruise missiles, and advanced air-to-surface weapons.[20] Another major ongoing construction effort has been the Expeditionary Combat Support Campus that is expected to further enhance Andersen's capacity to support major air operations in the region.[21] Since 2004, Guam has been hosting B-2 and B-52 bomber aircraft and F-15 and F-22 fighter jets on a rotational basis.[22] Six *Global Hawk* UAVs were permanently stationed at Andersen, alongside tankers and navy helicopters. Since 2005, piers at Apra Harbor on the west coast of the island were extended to berth transiting aircraft carriers and four attack submarines, 'required to track China's SSBN [emerging nuclear-powered and -armed submarines] capability'.[23] In addition, the Pentagon decided to deploy an Army Ballistic Missile Defense (BMD) task force alongside advanced radar detection systems. The enhanced capacity of Guam and its location close to the Asian continent gives the US more flexibility in deploying joint-force capabilities in the region, without the political constraints that exist in Japan and South Korea.

In Japan, bases have been restructured to maintain military readiness. Kadena Air Force Base in Okinawa, only 600 kilometres from mainland China and Taiwan, remains the largest of its kind overseas. It counts up to 70 F-15s as well as KC-135 tanker aircraft and various intelligence-gathering aircraft. Yokosuka naval base is the homeport of the US Navy's only permanently forward-deployed aircraft carrier. In 2007, a forward operational joint task-force headquarters was opened at Camp Zama, which is expected to operate closely with a newly constructed rapid-response headquarters of the Japanese Ground Self Defense Forces at the same site.[24] Likewise, the headquarters of the Fifth Air Force at Yokota Air Force Base will be modernised and deployed side-by-side with the Japanese Air Defense Command, with the aim to boost intelligence exchange and joint operations coordination. In 2006, an X-band radar installation, worth $2bn, was opened at Shariki and in 2008 a Joint Tactical Ground Station (JTAGS) in Misawa started to track ballistic missiles and to share radar data with Japanese and American onshore and offshore platforms.[25]

Apart from these three maritime hubs, America is maintaining several other stepping stones in the Pacific Rim. In the

ROK, the American military presence has been concentrated in Camp Humphreys in Pyeongtaek and Osan Air Force Base, an operation costing up to $10bn.[26] Since 2004, the US forces in Korea have been strengthened with new systems like the M1A1 *Abrams* battle tank, *Apache* attack helicopters, rotating *Stryker* brigade combat teams (mechanised infantry), UAV, equipment for one heavy armoured brigade on ships off the Korean coast, advanced U-2 reconnaissance planes, precision air-to-surface guided weapons, and the *Patriot* air-defence system.[27] Seoul and Washington decided to replace their current command structure with a new US–Korea Command (KORCOM), a sub-unified command of PACOM expected to be operational in 2011.[28] In Thailand, US forces were granted access to the Utapao Airport and the seaport of Sattahip for logistic transit to Iraq and Afghanistan.[29] In Singapore, Paya Lebar Air Force Base was assigned as a forward operating site (FOS) to host occasional rotational forces and contain pre-positioned material. Explaining the relevance of pre-positioning, a Congressional Report stated: 'When the Department of Defense places equipment on an ally's territory, it sends a message that the United States is willing to use force to protect that region from aggressors. Similarly... it signifies that US forces would probably also be allowed to operate there.'[30] In addition to these developments, the US has signed port-access agreements with other states such as Brunei, Indonesia and Malaysia.

The US retains its determination to secure its position as the major military power in East Asia by combining the deployment of superior systems with access to two tiers of modernised forward facilities. The wide range of conventional weapons in China's vicinity allows Washington the flexibility to use force at the various levels of war escalation, to limit China's strategic options, and to reassure its neighbours of America's credibility as an offshore balancer.

Yet, there are two indications that America's presence might not be that robust. Firstly, the US has been obliged to commit much of its force in the Pacific to the wars in Iraq and Afghanistan. One of the objectives of the Defense Posture Review was to make America's presence in Asia more suited for a wide array of operations within and outside the region. In 2001, the Pentagon decided to move away from the old threat-based strategy and to adopt a new capabilities-based approach: one that focuses less on who might threaten America, but more on how it might be threatened and what would be needed to defend against such threats. PACOM has indeed shown its adaptability by engaging various non-traditional challenges outside East Asia but, it transpired, at the cost of depleting its conventional deterrent. In 2004, 12 F-15s from Kadena and 12 F-16s from Misawa had to be temporarily deployed in Iraq.[31] In 2009, Washington ordered the deployment of the Fifth Stryker Brigade 2nd Division from Alaska and 8,000 Marines to Afghanistan, as well as all 24 *Apache* helicopters stationed in the ROK.[32] Between 2002 and 2008, 30,000 soldiers from PACOM were deployed in out-of-theatre operations. The Third Fleet's carrier battle groups also spent more time in the Arabian Gulf. As a consequence of the intensive deployment, wear-and-tear of key systems accelerated.

Secondly, US armed forces in the Pacific have increasingly been confronted with financial constraints. The economic crisis of 2008–09 aggravated these problems, with President Barack Obama instructing the Pentagon to cut its budget by 10%. Washington found it was unable to foot the entire bill of approximately $25bn for restructuring programmes already under way at its bases in Guam, Japan and the ROK. Consequently, in 2006 the Pentagon asked Tokyo to pay as much as $7.6bn for the relocation of US Marines to Guam.[33] After two years of bargaining, $6bn was approved by the Diet.[34] In 2010, the

Pentagon faced another setback, when Congress cut $300m from the budget for moving troops from Japan to Guam, fitting the island with new aircraft-carrier facilities and modernising its air defences. The Navy reported various difficulties meeting the objectives of its 30-year plan for modernising and replacing its major vessels. The submarine force reportedly executed just 54% of the requested mission days. Because of a lack of budget for new orders, the Navy predicted a decline in its total attack-submarine inventory from 51 to 41 by 2029.[35] Defense Secretary Gates also hinted that it would be too expensive to build a new generation of ballistic-missile submarines. For the same reason, the Navy warned that it was not able to replace one of its nuclear aircraft carriers by 2012 or to carry out necessary upgrades for its cruisers. It also said it would only procure three of the state-of-the-art *Zumwalt* destroyers, rather than 32 as originally planned.[36] Instead of the *Zumwalt*, the Pentagon decided to upgrade its *Arleigh Burke* destroyers and build a less expensive littoral combat ship.[37] Cuts to the *Raptor* procurement programme have also added to concerns about whether the US can meet its regional needs.[38]

Certainly, the US has maintained superior war-fighting capabilities deployed over the entire strategic depth of the Pacific Rim and, equally importantly, along the shipping lanes of the Indian Ocean. Its power-projection capacity in the region still comprises the most advanced military platforms, bases at strategic locations, and the most modern command, control, communication, information and intelligence (C4I2) facilities. Washington has tried to signal its resolve to sustain its dominance in the maritime margins of East Asia by deploying more troops to the region than to the European theatre, giving PACOM priority in the allocation of new armament and refurbishing its bases in the oceanic periphery around China. The US remains a potent military power, but military operations elsewhere, as well as financial restrictions, have narrowed its options. Its future military footprint in the Pacific has become to a large extent dependent on the the political willingness to invest in military presence far from home, and on the degree to which the US can succeed in maintaining its leading edge in military technologies. For the first time since the great wars of the last century, America has experienced increased constraints in balancing or deterring its main emerging military challenger. This has not been caused by political disinterest, but because shrinking material and financial resources started to affect its strategic manoeuvrability. Defense Secretary Gates said in a speech to the US Navy League Sea–Air–Space Expo in May 2010: 'I have in the past warned about our nation's tendency to disarm in the wake of major wars. That remains a concern. But, as has always been the case, defense budget expectations over time, not to mention any country's strategic strength, are intrinsically linked to the overall financial and fiscal health of the nation.'

Challenging America's maritime preponderance

China assumes that its future security and development cannot be guaranteed with an unpredictable hegemon impinging on its maritime sphere of interest.[39] Senior officers have vented this distrust on a regular basis. In 2009, retired PLA General Xu Guangyu questioned how the US would react if the shoe were on the other foot. He told the *South China Morning Post* that China's littorals were not the Gulf of Mexico, where the American Navy could enter and exit freely, and asked whether the US would accept Chinese incursions into its maritime periphery.[40] The same year, the *China Daily* quoted a former vice-commander of the PLAN saying: 'It's like a man with a criminal record wandering just outside the gate of a family home. When the host comes out to find out what he is doing there, the man complains that the host had violated his rights.'[41] These sentiments have also been echoed through official channels. The 2008 Defence White Paper, for example, said: 'Conflicting claims over territorial and maritime rights and interests remain serious, regional hotspots are complex. At the same time, the US has increased its strategic attention to and input in the Asia-Pacific region, further consolidating its military alliances, adjusting its military deployment and enhancing its military capabilities.'[42] In 2009, China's Defence Ministry said:

> China believes the constant US military air and sea surveillance and survey operations in China's exclusive economic zone had led to military confrontations between the two sides. The way to resolve China–US maritime incidents is for the US to change its surveillance and survey operations policies against China, decrease and eventually stop such operations.[43]

American dominance along China's coast inhibits the latter's ability to determine the outcome of an eventual conflict with Taiwan, to win wars with its neighbours over disputed territory, or to defend its industrial centres from Guangdong in the south all the way to Shandong in the north.[44] As long as America is the dominant power in the East Asian seas, China will not lay to rest memories of the colonial gunboats that heralded a century of despair and humiliation.

This persistent apprehension has been the main driver of China's strategising in the decades after the Cold War. Yet, the ambition to complete its transition from a peasant, agrarian society into a prosperous trading nation meant that moderation and patience were required in addressing US military preponderance. 'The conditions necessary for China to reach its development goal are a stable domestic environment and a peaceful international environment', Deng Xiaoping summarised in his famous 24-character dictum. It was he who underlined the need to 'observe and analyse developments calmly, deal with changes patient[ly] and confidently, secure our position, conceal our capacities and avoid the limelight, keep a low profile, never take the lead, and strive for achievements'.[45] Undoubtedly, there has been growing political and intellectual support for boosting China's naval power, but several opinion leaders have urged restraint. Ye Zicheng, an expert in Chinese diplomacy from Peking University's School of International Studies, said China's pursuit of maritime security should be gradual, so as not to offend the United States.[46] One of the original proponents of China's contemporary naval strategy, Zhang Wenmu, another professor at Peking University, said China should not risk provoking the US and other countries. 'The demise of all major powers in history has resulted from their succumbing to the temptation of excessive expansion,' he warned. Navy expert Liu Zhongmin even argued that the presence of the US Navy is not necessarily bad for China, as it safeguards the commercial sea lanes and dissuades other regional powers from building their own strong navies.[47] China's historical desire to secure its maritime periphery is thus tempered by strategic self-restraint.

In practice, this has meant that the PRC has set out to counter America's naval supremacy in the marginal waters of East Asia in a gradual and non-confrontational way. This cautious approach led Navy Commander Liu Huaqing in 1983 to sketch out a blueprint for tackling US preponderance along three strategic island chains step by step, putting China on a path to becoming a true ocean-going power by 2050. Two years later, the Central Military Commission approved the offshore defence strategy (*jinyang fangyu*) as the naval pillar of its active defence policy. In contrast to the earlier coastal defence (*jinan fangyu*) dictum, the new school of thought was that China could only defend itself if it engaged the enemy away from its shores.

> Overall, our military strategy is defensive and we attack only after being attacked. But our operations are offensive and space or time will not limit our counter-offensive ... We will wait for the time and conditions that favour our forces when we do initiate offensive operations and we will focus on the opposing force's weaknesses. Offensive operations against the enemy and defensive operations for our own force protection will be conducted simultaneously.[48]

This doctrine was upheld under Presidents Jiang Zemin and Hu Jintao, but both leaders stressed the goal of venturing further into the Pacific. In 1997, Jiang instructed the Navy to 'focus on enhancing its offshore comprehensive combat capabilities within the first island chain, increase nuclear and conventional deterrence and counterattack capabilities, and gradually develop combat capabilities for distant ocean defence'.[49] Hu stressed too that the Navy had to make headway in developing its ocean-going capabilities. In December 2004, he emphasised the task of the military was to safeguard China's expanding national interests, and highlighted the lack of military capabilities to defend those expanding interests and the gap between the current level of PLA capabilities and the aspiration to win a local war under informatised conditions, that is, requiring military units to share intelligence, have integrated communication, and joint command structures. In 2006, the White Paper on National Defence affirmed that 'The Navy aims at gradual extension of the strategic depth for offshore defensive operations and enhancing its capabilities in integrated maritime operations and nuclear counterattacks'.[50] Thus, China looks upon its desire to defend its maritime neighbourhood as a second manifest destiny in its security strategy, alongside its commitment to defend its continental borders and to regain control over Taiwan.

China's offshore defence strategy is built on deterrence. As the maritime counterpart of active defence, one of its main objectives is to avoid the cost of fighting a capable enemy within or close to China's borders, which requires that it possess a deterrence beyond its coastal waters. In his influential article on Chinese maritime strategy, Xu Qi wrote: 'The maritime security threat comes from the open ocean ... This requires the navy to cast the field of vision of its strategic defence to the open ocean and to develop attack capabilities for battle operations on exterior lines, in order to hold up the necessary shield for the long-term development of national interests'.[51] Authors such as Wang Xiaobin, an expert at the Beijing-based think tank China Academy of Social Science (CASS), have also highlighted the need to deal with long-range strikes from the high seas.[52] Nuclear force has been confirmed as the ultimate deterrent, but experts recognise that for the maritime balance to alter in China's favour, a whole range of military options should be available to flexibly deter aggressors and to respond properly to force escalation. In Chinese strategic thinking, deterrence combines incremental escalation and proportioned responses to an adversary's behaviour with asymmetrical escalations, so as to counter superior forces. *The Science of Military Strategy*, a major edited volume with contributions from leading PLA thinkers, defines deterrence as 'the military conduct of a state or political group in displaying force or showing the determination to use force to compel the enemy to submit to one's volition and to refrain from taking hostile actions or escalating the hostility'.[53] Most contingencies studied by Chinese scholars lead to two-tier deterrence scenarios: prevailing over the local challenger and dissuading US intervention. For defending its interests in its maritime periphery, China ultimately needs to keep America's supreme maritime might at bay, since the US could decide to influence China's decision-making by increasing its presence over the horizon, positioning its armed forces in the Taiwan Strait, or launching a counter-attack. Deterrence in the Pacific is thus seen as a means of equipping China for an offensive defence.[54]

Optimally, this capability has to be obtained at three levels.[55] It begins with access denial in a maritime zone that extends about 500km off China's coast and includes Taiwan, as well as most disputed islands in the East or South China Seas. Chinese armed forces should be able to inflict significant damage to major maritime and airborne platforms that penetrate this area, but also obstruct operations from forward locations like Okinawa. Another edited volume on military strategy, *The Science of Campaigns*, identifies the need to attack enemies' sea lanes in the deep sea as well as ports, docks and airports.[56] In the late 1990s, China relied mainly on conventional submarines and maritime bombers to carry out this task.[57] However, effective deterrence now demands the means to detect and engage hostile platforms that are able to stage long-range attacks – aircraft carriers with *Super Hornets* (combat radius 1,400–1,700km), surface combatants or submarines with *Tomahawk* cruise missiles (operational range 1,300–1,700km) – and to obstruct the use of Guam as a launch pad for aerial strikes.[58] Finally, China will need to guarantee the survivability of its nuclear forces against America's ever-improving anti-ballistic-missile systems.

In the case of conflicts in China's littoral zone, the challenge for Beijing is not to make sure that no enemy can get through, but rather to increase the opponent's vulnerability during its

Table 1. **Inventory of navy fleets**
Total number of vessels in service in 2000 (A), vessels in service in 2010 (B), and the number of new vessels planned or being built (if known) after 2010 (C).

	US PACOM			China			Japan			South Korea		
	A	B	C	A	B	C	A	B	C	A	B	C
Aircraft carrier CV/CVS	5	6	+1	0	0	-	0	0	-	0	0	-
Helicopter carrier or LPD* CVH/LHA/LHD/LPH/LPD	12	10	+6	0	1	+1	1	4	+1	0	1	+1
Cruiser C	13	12	-	0	0	-	0	0	-	0	0	=
Destroyer DD	24	32	+7	20	26	+1	42	42	+4	6	10	+1
Frigate FF	16	14	+2	40	52	+3	13	6	-	9	9	+6
Corvette FS	0	0	-	0	0	-	0	0	-	28	27	-
Conventional submarine SS/SSK	0	0	-	59	62	-	16	18	+4	8	12	+6
Nuclear submarine** SSN	30	34	+5	5	6	-	0	0	-	0	0	-
Ballistic Missile Submarine SSBN	8	8	-	1	3	-	0	0	-	0	0	-
Guided-missile patrol boat PCG/PBG	0	0	-	93	102	-	3	6	-	5	3	+6

	Russia Pacific			India			Australia			Vietnam		
	A	B	C	A	B	C	A	B	C	A	B	C
Aircraft carrier CV/CVS	0	0	-	1	1	+2	0	0	-	0	0	-
Helicopter carrier or LPD* CVH/LHA/LHD/LPH/LPD	0	0	-	0	1	-	0	0	+2	0	0	-
Cruiser C	1	1	-	0	0	-	0	0	-	0	0	-
Destroyer DD	7	7	-	8	8	+3	1	0	+3	0	0	-
Frigate FF	0	0	+4	12	10	+12	8	12	-	6	5	+2
Corvette FS	9	13	+5	19	24	+4	0	0	-	1	9	-
Conventional submarine SS/SSK	11	9	-	16	16	+6	3	6	-	0	0	-
Nuclear submarine** SSN	11	9	+6	0	0	+1	0	0	-	0	0	-
Ballistic Missile Submarine SSBN	5	5	+4	0	0	-	0	0	-	0	0	-
Guided-missile patrol boat PCG/PBG	27	10	-	6	0	-	0	0	-	12	8	-

* Landing platform dock. ** Nuclear submarines include ballistic-missile submarines.
In build refers to vessels ordered, launched but not commissioned and in various stages of construction.

strike missions to such a level that the costs of intervening become too high. Obstructing access to China's littoral waters and airspace is vital to preventing them from being used for attacking Chinese bombers or ships en route to their targets; for striking onshore installations; for staging anti-submarine operations; and for preventing blockades. This seems to be mission impossible. America has six nuclear aircraft carriers; China has none. The US deploys 12 guided-missile cruisers in the Pacific;

China has none. The US has 29 guided-missile destroyers in the region; China has only eight advanced ones. Add to that around 800 aircraft and a state-of-the-art C4I2 network, and it is tempting to conclude that China will not likely deter US intervention. Yet, this military balance is not static. As it develops new systems to catch up, China will become better able to threaten considerable damage to America's blue-water navy.

To start with, China is improving its long-range surveillance facilities, which are key to monitoring movements by hostile platforms. Since the late 1990s, several new systems have been widely applied. The indigenously produced JY-14 radar has a range of 590km, can track 100 targets and can feed the data to air-defence missile batteries. Since 2004, the YLC-2, the YLC-4 and the YLC-20 radars have been introduced. All have a detection range of more than 300km and and are claimed to have counter-stealth capabilities.[59] For detecting low-flying aircraft and ships, China is expanding its fleet of early warning and electronic intelligence aircraft.[60] It operates an increasing number of remote sensing satellites, such as the *YaoGan* class, which is able to detect and track moving targets in all weather conditions. Beijing has conceived plans to increase the coverage and performance of such satellites. The four *YaoGan* satellites that were put into orbit in 2010 are thought to be advanced high-resolution variants. These moves were consistent with a four-fold modernisation strategy sketched out in 2008 by a senior PLA officer. The strategy outlined the following priorities: stepping up offensive and defensive detection systems, enhancing joint tri-service and real-time processing, moving from a regional to an inter-continental early warning coverage and 'firepower information integration'.[61]

China has made a qualitative leap forward in developing new advanced platforms for denying access to navy ships. Between 2004 and 2008, it commissioned not less than ten new

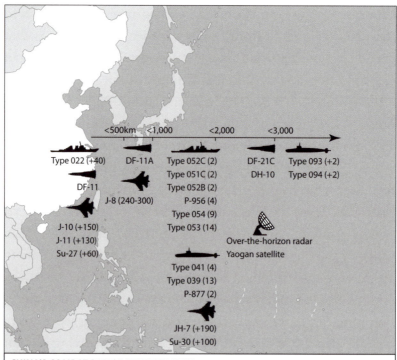

CHINA'S COMBAT RANGE IN THE PACIFIC

Basic overview of China's major weapon systems, their estimated number and range. Ranges (km): combat radius for aircraft, effective range for missiles, and approximate operational range in combat situations for ships.

BALLISTIC MISSILES

Type	Minimal range (km)	Number
DF-3A	3,000	17
DF-4	5,500	17
DF-5A	13,000	20
DF-11 and 11A	300–500	500–600
DF-15	500	300–350
DF-21	2,100	55
DF-31	7,200	10–15
DF-31A	11,200	10–15

*J-11 and Su-27 do not yet have a naval role but they could be assigned as interceptors over the Taiwan Straits

types of surface and subsurface combatants, amounting to a total of 85 new vessels.[62] Apart from conventional *Song*-class submarines, Type 054 frigates and the Type 022 fast-attack missile boats, most of them were produced in limited numbers. Despite the high costs of research and development, China had only deployed two of each of its new Type 052C and Type 051C destroyers by 2010. This is not because these ships were found to be inadequate: they have been successfully deployed far beyond China's shores. Rather, it is because of China's determination to use them as a test bed for new systems, and to move straight away to a more advanced generation. The same goes for the Type 093 *Shang*-class and Type 094 *Jin*-class nuclear submarines. These ships exposed China's growing ability to combine firepower with increasingly sophisticated C4I2 systems, and the gradual indigenisation of the production of such systems. In 2008 and 2009, various news reports stated that the 12th Five-Year Plan (2012–17) would include the launch of a new generation of multi-role destroyers, frigates and nuclear attack submarines.[63]

The PLAN is now able to engage surface combatants with various types of modern anti-ship missiles. Most recent surface combatants are equipped with the YJ-83, a supersonic sea-skimming missile with a range of 200km that can offer mid-course correction. For green-water contingencies, it can deploy more than 50 frigates of varying servicability and capability and more than 60 Type 022 fast-attack missile boats. The latter are small, stealthy catamaran vessels that carry eight YJ-83 missiles.[64] China has already deployed the YJ-62 sub-sonic long-range antiship missile, and is attempting to develop the YJ-12 rocket/ramjet with an even longer range, but the programme has experienced many delays and problems. While America's destroyers and cruisers are still more advanced than their Chinese counterparts, China is catching up, and in particular its growing fleet of frigates combined with a large number of Type 022s is already creating substantial risk for the US Navy to sail into potential conflict zones in East Asia.

The PLAN has added 25 modern conventional attack submarines to its fleet. All three generations commissioned between 2004 and 2008, the *Kilo*, the *Song* and the *Yuan*, have a relatively lower acoustic signature than some previous models and accurate sonar. Later models of the *Kilo* can launch new types of anti-ship missiles such as the Russian *Klub*-S, whereas the *Song* and the *Yuan* can launch encapsulated YJ-83 missiles. The latter is reported to be able to disable an aircraft carrier.[65] What adds specifically to the Chinese navy's advantage is its familiarity with the very shallow waters of the South and East China Seas.[66] Complex thermal layers, tide noise and the influx of water from rivers make it very difficult to detect pre-positioned submarines. Conventional diesel-electric submarines are ideal for navigating in such environments, and apart from the new *Virginia* class, older US or Japanese types lack the sophisticated detection capacities that are needed to operate in these areas. Moreover, in denial operations China is likely to deploy its submarines in conjunction with a large-scale use of sea-mines, which could complicate US anti-submarine warfare, certainly because the US Navy has limited mine-sweeping capabilities.[67] China's new submarines could thus substantially raise the cost for enemies to deploy their submarines against Chinese surface combatants. They also limit the manoeuvrability of superior surface combatants to hunt their Chinese counterparts.

China is also harnessing its military to project air power into its maritime periphery. In 2004, the navy's air force (PLANAF) obtained about 60 improved JH-7A maritime bombers that are able to launch the YJ-83. That year it also received 24 *Sukhoi-30MK2* (Su-30), a world-class, long-range maritime strike aircraft able to detect and engage several targets at the same time. Since 2000, the army air force (PLAAF) has been modernised with about 660 new fighter. These modern aircraft consist of either the Russian *Sukhoi*-27 multi-role fighter or the Chinese J-10. Some 200 or more of its modern craft are Su-30MKK and J-11. China's new fighters are equipped with increasingly capable air-to-air missiles on a par with most advanced air forces. The PL-12, for example, is a guided air-to-air missile with multiple-target engagement capability, comparable to the American AIM-120 advanced medium-range air-to-air missile (AMRAAM) in performance. The Russian R-77 (AA-12 *Adder*) is an active radar-homing, all-weather, medium-range air-to-air missile. The missile is 'fire-and-forget', which enables several missiles to be fired simultaneously at multiple targets. Pilots who fly the most modern aircraft are receiving more and more specialised training for all-weatther operations above sea or at night, practise more in simulators and are beginning to address the superiority of their US counterparts in terms of training hours.[68] Moreover, whereas joint operations used to be problematic, it has become common to organise integrated manoeuvres. China operates more than 2,000 second- and third-generation fighters, but amid this fleet of ageing machines a modern and well-trained combat force is emerging that can be increasingly deployed to guard China's littoral security perimeter.

This air power is supported by various new air-defence systems. China operates 160 Russian S-300s, as well as a large number of domestically produced HQ-9 and HQ-15 surface-to-air missile launchers. The latest variants can target aircraft at 200km and incoming cruise missiles at a distance of 50km. The two Type 051C and two Type 052C destroyers, and six Type 054A frigates, all commissioned between 2004 and 2008, mark China's objective to develop fleet defence against airborne threats, such as vertical launching systems for either S-300 or HQ-9 missiles and medium-range surface-to-air missiles. Whereas the air-defence missiles of the Type 052 *Luhu*-class destroyers commissioned in the mid-1990s only had a reach of about 13km, the Type 051C *Luzhou*-class destroyer is able to engage six airborne targets simultaneously beyond 80km.[69] The Type 052C *Lanzhou* destroyer, commissioned in 2005, demonstrates the advancing detection capacity of China's navy. Its active phased-array radar, which is able to track targets and guide missiles, has a detection range of 450km.[70] The Type 054A frigate's air-defence system can trace 40 targets simultaneously at a maximum range of 120km.[71] Most of these vessels are equipped with the Russian *Fregat*-MAE-5 3D air-search radar, but the *Aegis*-like radar installed on the Type 052C also shows China's successful attempt to develop its own advanced radar systems.

China has improved its ability to carry out preventive strikes against air bases in its vicinity. Bases on the southern islands of Japan are within firing range of short-range ballistic missiles.[72] The DF-15 has been re-designed specifically with a view to striking facilities beyond Taiwan. The result, the DF-15A, mainly deployed in Jiangxi province, has a range of 700km to 1,000km. The accuracy of its delivery, referred to as Circular Error Probable (CEP), improved from 150–500 metres for earlier versions to only 30m for the DF-15A, and its higher terminal velocity makes it more difficult to intercept by guided missile air-defence systems like the PAC-2 and PAC-3. Chinese experts have widely discussed the use of conventional DF-15As against US bases in Okinawa and Japanese surveillance installations in the East China Sea.[73]

Beijing has also increased its command-and-control capabilities. In the past, the Chinese armed forces were known for their slow and hierarchic command structures. Since the beginning of the twenty-first century, the PLA has carried out various reforms to decentralise tactical command and control to local commanders and joint battle commands.[74] This has been continuously tested and evaluated through various innovative large-scale exercises with tactical joint commands and real-time exchange of information between different components and platforms between 2004 and 2008.[75] American, Japanese and Taiwanese forces still have the edge in this field, but China has made C4I2 a priority in its military modernisation. While all recent military systems display enhanced platform-centric warfare, the PLA has started to make progress in enhancing network-centric warfare technologies.[76] Domestically produced data-link systems now allow real-time information exchange between China's navy, air force and ground forces.[77] The recent types of the destroyers, for example, are equipped with ZKJ-4A and H/ZBJ-1 combat information centres that offer joint-tactical data linkage and friend-or-foe recognition.[78]

Gradually, China is taking steps towards increasing its presence in the South China Sea. In 2007 a new navy base was opened near to Sanya, Hainan. This facility, only 300km from the Paracel Islands, has long piers for hosting a large fleet of warships, and a new underground base for submarines.[79] Further south, China maintains smaller facilities on Woody Island, Fiery Cross Reef and Mischief Reef. Satellite imagery shows various electronic systems. Woody Island, located in the centre of the South China Sea, comprises seven large radars, a long pier and a runway more than 3km long. There have been reports that China has developed a network of maritime hubs (a 'String of Pearls'), that stretches from the South China Sea to Hambantota in Sri Lanka and the Pakistani port of Gwadar.[80] While it is possible that China has increased its commercial linkages with these places, there is as yet no evidence that it is using them as naval hubs or for maritime surveillance.[81] Indeed, Sri Lankan Navy Commodore Ravindra Wijegunaratne has denied the claims, saying: 'Sri Lanka is a pearl, but it will never be a part of a Chinese string. India remains our main military partner. Yes we got Chinese weapons to fight the Tamil tigers, but that does not make [a] difference.'[82] Interestingly, China has refrained from establishing a military base near to the Gulf of Aden, where it has been operating against pirates since 2008. The PLAN appears to have called on different ports and worked with civilian suppliers rather than establishing an outpost.[83] A retired Chinese officer explained that this was mainly to downplay suspicion, but that military leaders were still lobbying to establish military hubs in the long term, on the grounds that the current logistical organisation would not be enough to support larger missions, that onshore facilities are needed to maintain the crews on the Chinese warships in good condition, and that China should have the right, like any other power, to build such hubs.[84] Japan, meanwhile, has announced that it will set up a military logistical hub in this area.

Lastly, China is developing new means to deter distant strikes. Since 2003, Chinese experts have intensively discussed the relevance of the DF-21 ballistic missile against slow-moving targets.[85] The DF-21 is a land-based, intermediate-range ballistic missile with a range of approximately 2,500km that probably combines a conventional manoeuvrable re-entry vehicle with terminal guidance. It is estimated that the missile can travel at Mach-10 and reach 2,500km in less than 15 minutes. While its use against maritime targets has not been tested, it is assumed that China's over-the-horizon radar can detect distant platforms. *YaoGan* satellites can provide additional tracking data and after launch a combination of global positioning and radar seekers will guide the warhead to its target.[86] Although it is not certain whether the Chinese have been able to perfect the system, if they can produce it successfully, it will mark a significant leap forward in the PLA's technical capacity.[87] The PLA has produced long-range cruise missiles with a range of 1,500–2,000km. In 2004 it reportedly carried out a first test with the DH-10 cruise missile.[88] Making use of Russian, American or Chinese global-positioning systems, the DH-10 would be capable of targeting facilities at Guam, but also slow-moving targets offshore. While cruise missiles are slower and can therefore be more easily eliminated by defence systems when deployed in large numbers, they can still form a potent threat. China's cruise-missile programme is highly secretive; what discussion there is within the country often appears to be a reflection of Western reports. The DH-10 was, however, publicly displayed during the military parade of October 2009 to mark the 60th anniversary of the PRC.

In a 2010 article in the *Liberation Army Daily*, retired Major General Xu Guangyu stated that China should 'convince the other side that it faces an intolerable second-strike nuclear capability' and that China will continue to improve the survivability of its missiles.[89] It is indeed making progress in modernising its nuclear deterrence and turning the Second Artillery Corps into a reliable deterrent. The survivability of its nuclear forces is being enhanced by introducing an upgraded road-mobile launch platform for the solid-fuel DF-21 intermediate-range ballistic missile. In 2003, the Second Artillery Corps started introducing the DF-31 intercontinental ballistic missile. It features solid-fuel motors and can be transported over road and railway. In 2002, China reportedly carried out the first successful experiment with decoys and multiple independently targetable re-entry vehicles (MIRV), which makes ballistic-missile defence more challenging.[90] Thus far, however, it is not known whether this system is actually fitted on Chinese missiles. Another way to promote survivability has been to maintain quantitative ambiguity. Whereas China adheres to a policy of minimal deterrence and operates a small number of missiles compared to the United States, it is not known how many, how and where these vehicles are deployed. To enhance its second-strike capability, China introduced the *Jin*-class ballistic-missile submarine, which was to be fitted with a modified variant of the DF-31, the *Julang*-2 two-stage, solid-fuel missile. A first test with the *Julang*-2 in

2010 failed, but the PLA remained committed to improving the vehicle. Additionally, in 2009, Chinese state broadcaster CCTV 7 reported the completion of the so-called 'underground Great Wall' (*dixia changcheng*), a network of more than 2,500km of tunnels in Hebei province built to house the PRC's nuclear arsenal. Pictures show an advanced system of large shafts with railways, oxygen systems and subsoil control rooms, which would certainly make launch platforms less vulnerable in case of a strike.[91]

Another important factor that will add to China's deterrence is its assumed capability in terms of electronic warfare. Integrated network and electronic warfare (*wangdian yitizhan*) has figured prominently in China's recent strategic thinking. An article in the *Liberation Army Daily* stated: 'In future high-tech warfare, offensive operations will often require to first destroy the enemy's integrated battlefield command- and control-systems and warfare networks ... [and] to attack its state or military communication hubs, financial centres and C4ISER systems, so as to directly affect the enemy's strategic decision making'.[92] The main aim is thus to paralyse the challenger's firepower and to weaken its domestic support base. China reportedly has given hints that it can penetrate the civilian and military information systems of other countries, and has also visibly invested in new combat systems. It has started to deploy J-7 interceptor and J-8 fighter aircraft, and ships equipped with installations to disturb communication from adversaries. It also started to develop anti-satellite capability. Electronic warfare is considered a deterrence multiplier. The lack of information, particularly about China's true capacity in this area, will raise the threshold for others to risk military escalation.

The transition of China's military power in its green waters and in the high seas of the Pacific is bound to erode America's traditional maritime preponderance. True, the US is ahead of China when it comes to the number and quality of major surface combatants and nuclear submarines. US armed forces have far more advanced C4I2 and can take advantage of the strategic depth of the Pacific Ocean thanks to US blue-water naval power-projection capabilities and bases scattered across the region. But China might not need to aim at the same kind of maritime power to discourage American intervention, should a war break out over Taiwan or claims in the East and South China Seas. China is continuing to improve its littoral defences by investing in advanced platforms and by training its troops in joint warfare under high-tech conditions. Its impressive fleet of fast missile-attack ships and its increasing number of conventional attack submarines might not be as overwhelming as America's aircraft battle groups; they are nonetheless lethal enough to defend China's interests in a limited area. In an armed contingency in the Chinese periphery, the risks for American fighter jets or patrol aircraft would be significant because of China's rapidly growing onshore and offshore air-defence missiles, early warning systems, and large fleet of modern interceptors like the latest *Sukhoi* variants. Anti-submarine warfare, still one of the main comparative advantages of the US (certainly if it joins forces with Japan), could be deterred by the exposure of patrol aircraft to China's air defence, the lack of capability to protect surface ships against advanced mobile sea mines, China's own surface combatants, and the difficulty of tracking prepositioned conventional submarines in shallow waters. The US distant offshore presence in the western Pacific too will probably become more vulnerable to the new asymmetric threats, but America will maintain the ability to use its Pacific forces to stage attacks with cruise missiles launched by submarines or by aircraft out of range of China's air defence. Thus, China is capable of substantial access denial against an

American intervention in China's green waters. But will it be enough to reassure China?

Towards a new military equilibrium in the Asia-Pacific?

China has not only started improving its littoral defences; it has also made its first strides in the development of offshore defence capabilities. For decades it has been aiming at overcoming Taiwan's technological edge and dissuading the US from sailing into the narrow Taiwan Strait in times of war. The challenge in that regard was to beef up firepower, while ensuring that technologically superior enemies could not cut off an eventual strike. Guided by the concept of limited warfare under high-tech conditions, Beijing has developed a niche force that underwent rapid modernisation to function in this specific theatre. China's denial capacity has been enhanced by positioning silent conventional submarines in the shallow waters around Taiwan and by deploying a large fleet of rather small surface combatants like the Type 022 missile-attack ship or the Type 054 frigate family. Various new generations of multi-role fighters and intensive training for elite units also increased China's air-denial capacity. This leap forward coincided with improved C4I2 facilities and growing emphasis on joint-warfare scenarios. Obviously, such capabilities can also be deployed beyond the Taiwan Strait. Since 2003, large joint-force manoeuvres staged in the South and East China Seas highlighted China's growing maritime power in the East Asian green waters. In April 2010, it conducted two large, almost simultaneous exercises, in addition to dispatching three ships in the Gulf of Aden. In the first of these, a large flotilla of the North Sea Fleet sailed through the Bashi Strait between the Philippines and Taiwan, while a major confrontation exercise was staged in the Spratly archipelago, flanked by combat aircraft from different airfields that tested their night-flying skills, mid-air refuelling, radar jamming and simulated bombing raids. Almost at the same time, a flotilla of 12 ships from the East Sea Fleet, including two submarines, sailed through international waters between Okinawa and Miyako into the Pacific with helicopters practising close surveillance of Japanese ships. These bold operations clearly showed the PLAN's growing ability to stage integrated operations and its intent to protect its core interests beyond the first island chain. China has started to alter the naval balance in this area, which it not only sees as a legitimate part of its territory but also as a first line of defence against intruders. It has achieved this by deploying cost-effective, sea-based weapons systems backed up by numerically overwhelming and technologically enhanced onshore strike power.

The question, then, is whether China is satisfied with this changing balance and, consequently, whether Washington will tolerate it. Several Chinese and American strategists have emphasised that maintaining security in the Pacific should not be seen as a zero-sum game and that both sides would benefit from cooperation. One of the most significant factors in preventing the US and China from becoming entangled in military competition is the strong economic interconnections that bind the two countries. Trans-Pacific relations are characterised by commercial linkages, not military divisions. However, it is also argued that security interdependence may help guarantee stability. American commanders such as former PACOM chief Timothy Keating have stressed that it should not be a problem that China wants a bigger role on the world stage, because its globalising security interest would facilitate global military cooperation.[93] Many observers have highlighted America's offer to work with the PLAN in the context of the multilateral anti-piracy operation in the Gulf of Aden in 2008 as a clear expression of the potential for new synergies. Moreover, it can be assumed that now that China has attained the capacity to deter interference in the Taiwan Strait and to sanction any regional country that would challenge its maritime territorial interests, it may feel secure enough to refrain from further maritime expansion. In addition, both sides face economic constraints. America will have to constrain its defence spending because of its economic problems, while China too will have to prioritise domestic development, but to a lesser degree. This restraint would be further promoted by the large number of security challenges that China faces within and outside its continental borders.

Yet, there are two indications that a naval arms race could be on the horizon. Firstly, China still finds that it needs to engage America's naval supremacy in the high seas of the Pacific and is starting to develop new capabilities. Secondly, for the US, the ability to show force in China's green waters is essential to demonstrate its resolve as a military balancer and also to keep its own first line of defence tightened to the shores of its immediate contender.

In the context of its offshore defence thinking, China still feels that it will have to develop new means to ward off an eventual US strike. In spite of its increasing power in the Asian maritime margins, it understands that the US does not have to pass China's emerging Great Wall at sea to attack Chinese targets. Beyond the littoral, the next maritime security frontier for China stretches about 2,500km from its shores, at and around Guam. Within this area, long-range strike-fighters could pose a threat to China. Cruise missiles can be launched to strike military bases in coastal provinces. Defensive measures do not suffice to answer this threat. It would be nearly impossible operationally to ward off a sustained missile attack and air strikes without eliminating the distant launch platforms.[94] The only effective defence in this regard is to go on the offensive, and this does demand blue-water naval capabilities. Apart from a small number of destroyers and frigates, China does not yet have such capacity. Neither are its few Su-30MK2 maritime bombers a match for America's fighters or air-defence systems. An even larger dilemma has been the American preponderance in the Indian Ocean. Even leaving aside the question of how significant the American military presence is in the Pacific and the Indian Ocean, with the latter being less of a concern, Chinese experts recognise that the US Navy could reciprocate China's progress in sea denial in East Asia with its maritime deterrence in South Asia.

Thus far, China has opted for asymmetric deterrence. Cruise missiles and modified ballistic missiles are China's first answer to distant surface combatants or forward bases. As we have seen in previous sections, Beijing has sought to overcome its naval inferiority in the blue waters of the Pacific with an arsenal of missiles. In the long history of naval warfare, China's adapted DF-21 might well become the most capable answer of a continental power to challenge the maritime superiority of its rival. In the same vein, new generations of long-range land-attack sea-skimming cruise missiles could form a potent threat to facilities within the second island chain. But DF-21 missiles bring the risk that the enemy will not be able to distinguish between conventional and nuclear types in the initial launch stages and may order a nuclear counter-strike.[95] Advanced cruise missiles are more vulnerable to defence measures. Moreover, China would still face America's attack submarines as platforms for launching cruise missiles. The 31 *Los Angeles-* and *Virginia*-class subs in the Pacific could carry a total of 372 cruise missiles. This represents a rather modest firepower compared to America's cruisers or destroy-ers, and it is not likely that its submarines will be exclusively deployed for land-attack operations. Is China able to engage a more superior enemy in view of these limitations? Given the fact that China's conventional submarines are more effective in its green waters, and that it does not have sufficient airborne anti-submarine warfare capacity, this only leaves its two recent Type 093 nuclear attack submarines. Leaving aside the technical inferiority of these systems compared to the *Los Angeles* class, their small number and China's limited experience in long-range operations mean they are no match for America's submarine force.

Senior officials, prominent scholars and military experts have repeatedly stated that China's military development does not end at the first island chain, which stretches from the Kuril Islands and Japan, through Taiwan and the Philippines. One leading scholar stated:

> China will not change its peaceful development approach but it will make strides in hard-power areas too by patrolling the Somali coast, building large aircraft, and constructing aircraft carriers. China's military goal is still to overcome the Seventh Fleet. The US will selectively have to accept China to become a leader in some security areas. It will have to recognize the mutual balance of deterrence in Asia and in the Strait of Taiwan in particular.[96]

In describing the US forward military presence in East Asia, most Chinese experts claim that it is pursuing a new kind of maritime containment, and that China should address this vulnerability. This perception has been strengthened because of Washington's perseverance in maintaining its Asian strongholds, despite the financial constraints and military overstretch caused by its missions in Iraq and Afghanistan.[97] Jiang Yuanqing and Zou Hui have posited that China should prepare for a Cold

War at sea.[98] Various colleagues have found evidence of this prospect in America's 'naval encroachments' under the banner of freedom of navigation, in the recent transformation of Guam into one of the largest military strongholds abroad, and in the decision of the US to deploy its latest equipment first in the Pacific, and even to showcase these platforms in exercises with China's neighbours.[99] Hu Xin said:

> China's most important security challenges are likely to come from the sea … The US Navy is adjusting to the 'China threat' by sending more advance[d] aircraft carriers, attack submarines and other offensive equipment to the western Pacific, which is a serious threat to the region's peace and stability. Distrust, power politics and nationalism will bring about Asian 'waters of instability'.[100]

Another author stated ominously that from Okinawa or Guam it takes only 20 minutes to fly F-22s to the Taiwan Strait.[101]

While there is a general agreement that the PLA should continue to prepare for a potential confrontation with the US, there are different opinions about how much it should, therefore, venture into the wide open of the Pacific Ocean or about the degree of restraint that it should show in its attempts to catch up.[102] Conservatives believe that China is essentially a continental power, and therefore that it should refrain from maritime adventurism. Ye Zicheng, for instance, has called for land power to be prioritised over sea power. He argues that China can engage maritime threats by boosting the performance of land-based guided missiles and aircraft.[103] Conservatives often highlight that China will probably never be able to deal with sea-denial contingencies west of the Malacca Strait. Naval expansionists maintain that because of growing trade and the concentration of wealth along the coastline, China is becoming a maritime nation, and should adapt its strategies accordingly. China's rise, they argue, can only be secured if it is able to prevent sea-denial activities beyond its green waters.[104] Some scholars argue that such ventures should be cooperative and avoid confrontation, and, therefore, that they should be embedded in expanded exchanges with the US.[105]

Naval expansionists say that any blue-water naval capacity in the end boils down to the ability to take out US submarines and surface combatants. Building a large fleet of nuclear submarines is one of the proposals, but another is the development of aircraft-carrier battle groups, and more advanced missiles that are able to break through the US's improving defence systems, or to 'hack out a path through the thorns and thistles', as a leading scholar at the National Defense University put it the *Liberation Army Daily*.[106] How would this take into account the Indian Ocean dilemma? The most common argument is that, by dominating the sea lanes east of the Malacca Strait, China would deter hostile naval operations in South Asia as well.[107] One expert at the China Institute for International Strategic Studies claimed that the best way to tackle the conundrum was to combine offshore deterrence in the east with the expansion of supply lines onshore in the west.[108] However, it appears that this linkage between the eastern and southern maritime front has not yet been thought through, and that the discussion has not yet fully crystallised into policy options.

What is clear is that the Chinese government has decided to expand its blue-water navy capacity. It showed its growing confidence in the development of a strong ocean-going navy. In 2008, for example, President Hu inspected the PLAN's new base in Sanya, Hainan, and reiterated the Navy's responsibility to defend China's expanding security interests.[109] In November 2008, the Chinese government announced the deployment of a flotilla near Somalia, its first out-of-area naval operation for 600 years. In April 2009, it held a substantial naval parade that flaunted many of its modern submarines and destroyers. Simultaneously, it started organising bolder and more demanding manoeuvres in its littoral waters, and showed more vigilance in responding to American patrols in its maritime periphery.[110] The most compelling evidence, however, is that China is investing heavily in major arms-development programmes. Even if media reports that the PLAN is constructing two to five modern variants of the Type 093 submarine can be verified, this will not fundamentally affect America's leading edge in the blue waters of the Pacific. What is more significant is that work on various systems for a new advanced generation of nuclear attack submarines, combined with surface anti-submarine warfare, has provided a foundation for future technological breakthrough. The PRC one of the few countries that has mastered the technology for producing very small but powerful nuclear reactors, and has experimented with indigenously designed sonar systems and pump-jet or magneto-hydrodynamic propulsion systems.[111] In the same vein, China is investing in the development of a true blue-water navy surface fleet that will include modern surface combatants and aircraft carriers. The new destroyers and frigates that were mentioned in earlier sections could obviously play a role, but to date, they have been mainly assigned to provide air defence and fire power close to China's shores. In addition, the number of these new vessels has been kept very low. In the case of the Type 051 and Type 052 family of destroyers, only two hulls of each type were commissioned.

Yet, these small numbers by no means imply that China has no ambition to expand and improve its surface fleet. China follows a leapfrog (*kuayue*) policy. While learning lessons from the few new vessels, research centres have continued to conceive

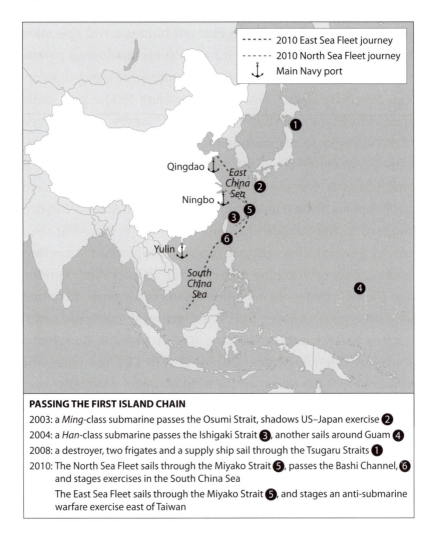

PASSING THE FIRST ISLAND CHAIN

2003: a *Ming*-class submarine passes the Osumi Strait, shadows US–Japan exercise ❷

2004: a *Han*-class submarine passes the Ishigaki Strait ❸, another sails around Guam ❹

2008: a destroyer, two frigates and a supply ship sail through the Tsugaru Straits ❶

2010: The North Sea Fleet sails through the Miyako Strait ❺, passes the Bashi Channel, ❻ and stages exercises in the South China Sea

The East Sea Fleet sails through the Miyako Strait ❺, and stages an anti-submarine warfare exercise east of Taiwan

new models and to do so with more indigenously developed systems. In April 2009, Navy Commander Wu Shengli stated: 'We have accelerated the pace of building weapons and equipment, the development of large surface combat ships, self-sustainable and well performing new stealth submarines, supersonic combat aircraft, accurate long-range missiles, torpedoes'.[112] In November 2009, the Commander of the PLAAF said work was under way on a fifth-generation air-superiority fighter. Even if a small number of these were operational by

2020, as reported by unverified Chinese media sources, they would be significantly outnumbered by US F-22s.[113] Working under tight security, China is taking its time to experiment with prototypes and to indigenise the production of key technologies, and is therefore not likely to overcome US superiority in the short term.

The United States has nevertheless received news of developments with growing concern. The blueprints for the consolidation of its presence in East Asia were already sketched out before China started to assert its desire to extend the range of its offshore defence, and before the entry of new advanced systems that could be deployed against American targets in the region.[114] The official posture of the Pentagon became that the US would accept the PRC's maritime ambitions as a reflection of its rise in world affairs. In return China was expected to reveal its long-term intentions and to respect freedom of navigation, even in disputed areas of the South and East China Seas. Apart from the issue of transparency, which has always been on Washington's agenda, the Department of Defense gradually became more critical in its analysis of China's naval modernisation, which was beginning to appear increasingly at odds with its stated peaceful objectives. In testimony before the House Armed Services Committee in December 2007, the Chief of Naval Operations Admiral Gary Roughead said the rate at which China was building up its attack-submarine fleet and anti-access and area denial weapons was a concern. During an exchange with the Admiral, Representative Duncan Hunter said: 'With respect to the increased production, in terms of them outstripping us by three-to-one on submarine production – and your own figures show that they are going to eclipse us in submarine numbers in 2011 – maybe a little earlier, maybe a little later ... clearly, that should be a concern to you'. Roughead replied: 'well, it is.'[115]

For its part, China has grown weary of repeated charges that it does not share information, and has become more vocal in questioning why it should not be allowed to build carriers when the US may do so without raising any eyebrows. PACOM Commander Timothy Keating relayed this mounting sense of injustice in testimony to Congress in 2008. Broadly paraphrasing a Chinese naval counterpart, he said: 'We're going to start building aircraft carriers. You guys can have the east part of the Pacific, Hawaii to the states,' he quoted. 'You keep your aircraft carriers east of Hawaii. We'll keep ours west. You share your information with us and we'll share our information with you. We'll save you the time and effort of coming all the way to the western Pacific.'[116]

In 2009, Admiral Michael Mullen, the Chairman of the Joint Chiefs of Staff, publicly stated that China was 'developing capabilities that are very maritime focused, maritime and air focused, and in many ways they seem very focused on the US Navy and our bases that are in that part of the world'.[117] The same month, Defense Secretary Gates made an unusually direct reference to China's threat in the Pacific in a speech at the Naval War College.

> I might also note that we have a number of expeditionary strike groups and will, in the not-too-distant future, be able to carry the F-35. Potential adversaries are well aware of this fact, which is why, despite significant naval modernization programs under way in some countries, no one intends to bankrupt themselves by challenging the US to a shipbuilding competition akin to the Dreadnought arms race prior to World War I. Instead, we have seen their investments in weapons geared to neutralize our advantages: to deny the US military freedom of movement and action while

potentially threatening our primary means of project-
ing power: our bases, sea and air assets, and the
networks that support them.[118]

In May 2010, Gates sounded even more concerned. 'The virtual
monopoly the US has enjoyed with precision guided weapons
is eroding,' he said. 'The US will also face increasingly sophisticated underwater combat systems – including numbers of
stealthy subs – all of which could end the operational sanctuary
our Navy has enjoyed in the western Pacific for the better part of
six decades.'[119] Such statements should not be dismissed merely
as alarmist pleas for getting more out of the government's
shrinking budget. Public perceptions of China as a military threat
are increasingly common too.[120] These views could become even
more negative should America lose confidence in its military
clout because of the wars in Iraq and Afghanistan, while China
more assertively showcases its own military prowess.

Interaction between Chinese and US armed forces remains
problematic. On the one hand, US officials complain that
cooperation with the PRC regarding international security
challenges has not met their expectations. In case of the nuclear
ambitions of Iran and North Korea, both sides continue to be at
loggerheads over the relevance of sanctions. Beijing declined to
consider active support to the stabilisation of Afghanistan. On
the other hand, American officials and experts have insisted
that the PLA has become more assertive in signalling its aversion to America's military presence in the region. The American
weapon sales to Taiwan in 2008 and 2010 were followed by
harsh statements from Beijing and a temporary ban on military relations. China had already begun to demonstrate its
emerging capabilities, staging in January 2007 a successful
test of a ground-based, anti-satellite missile, which targeted
and destroyed one of its ageing weather satellites. This drew

immediate protests from other nations with satellite technology, as the resulting debris cloud could have damaged their systems. In 2009, China 'harassed' US Navy surveillance vessels six times in its exclusive economic zone (EEZ).[121]

For the US, these surveillance missions were a matter of pressuring China to be transparent in its military transition and stressing the freedom of navigation in the EEZ. China's riposte was that the US should make its intentions more transparent. It also maintained that it was not against freedom of navigation, but that it opposed offensive military posturing, and that Washington should not interfere with the territorial disputes between China and other Asian countries. Further offshore, incidents between Chinese submarines and American surface combatants have become an almost annual phenomenon. While the US showed its resolve by dispatching aircraft-carrier battle groups, China responded by dispatching its submarines, often even at torpedo range. In November 2006, a Chinese *Song*-class submarine surfaced within five miles of the USS *Kitty Hawk* carrier group in ocean waters near Okinawa. In November 2007, another *Song* was detected near the *Kitty Hawk* in the Taiwan Strait. The group was en route to Japan after China refused its port call in Hong Kong. In November 2008, two Chinese submarines, including a *Han*-class nuclear-powered attack submarine, were discovered around the time that the aircraft carrier USS *George Washington* was operating near the ROK. In June 2009, a submarine hit the towed sonar array of an *Arleigh Burke*-class destroyer in the South China Sea.

Again, for many American spectators this was evidence that China was becoming more self-confident in trying to keep the US out of its green waters. Strong statements of senior Chinese officers fuelled this suspicion. At the US-China Strategic and Economic Dialogue in 2010, for example, Admiral Guan Youfei accused the US of plotting to encircle China with strategic

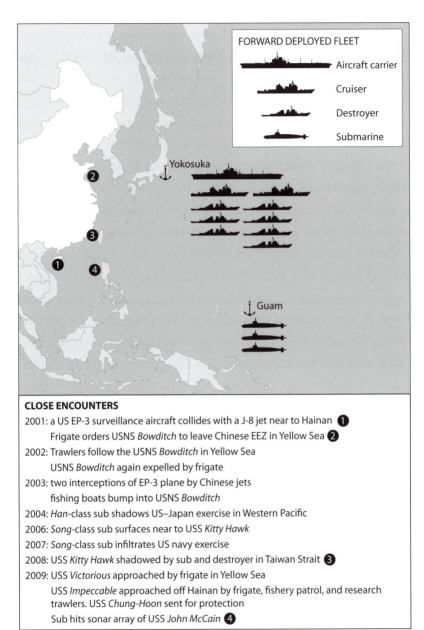

FORWARD DEPLOYED FLEET

Aircraft carrier

Cruiser

Destroyer

Submarine

Yokosuka

Guam

CLOSE ENCOUNTERS

2001: a US EP-3 surveillance aircraft collides with a J-8 jet near to Hainan ❶

Frigate orders USNS *Bowditch* to leave Chinese EEZ in Yellow Sea ❷

2002: Trawlers follow the USNS *Bowditch* in Yellow Sea

USNS *Bowditch* again expelled by frigate

2003: two interceptions of EP-3 plane by Chinese jets

fishing boats bump into USNS *Bowditch*

2004: *Han*-class sub shadows US–Japan exercise in Western Pacific

2006: *Song*-class sub surfaces near to USS *Kitty Hawk*

2007: *Song*-class sub infiltrates US navy exercise

2008: USS *Kitty Hawk* shadowed by sub and destroyer in Taiwan Strait ❸

2009: USS *Victorious* approached by frigate in Yellow Sea

USS *Impeccable* approached off Hainan by frigate, fishery patrol, and research trawlers. USS *Chung-Hoon* sent for protection

Sub hits sonar array of USS *John McCain* ❹

alliances. Less than ten days later at the Shangri-La Dialogue, Deputy Chief of Staff Ma Xiaotian hit out at US interlocutors for supplying arms to Taiwan and 'setting obstacles' to the development of military relations.[122]

This assertiveness was not new. Accusations of hegemony erupted in 1993 after the US Navy forced the freighter *Yin He* to stop in international waters, in 1996 during the Third Taiwan Strait crisis when two aircraft carriers were dispatched to the region in response to fears of an imminent Chinese invasion; and in 1999 when the Chinese Embassy in Belgrade was bombed by NATO forces. US surveillance activities in China's green waters drew similar allegations. When the cruiser USS *Vincennes* started a first undersea warfare training and data-collection mission in the South China Sea in 2000, Beijing expressed its concern. In 2001, the USNS *Bowditch* was repeatedly hounded out of China's EEZ in the Yellow, East China and South China Seas. The same year, these tensions culminated tragically in the collision between an American EP-3 surveillance aircraft and a Chinese J-8 interceptor jet over Hainan, which killed the Chinese pilot and sparked a diplomatic dispute. Hence, rather than growing assertiveness from China's side, it could be argued that China's military modernisation has prompted the US to show more resolve in using force posturing or strong public statements to pressure China to practise restraint, to become more transparent and to refrain from considering its EEZ as an exclusive sphere of military influence. Even though some of China's reactions were considered to be clumsy, the tit-for-tat highlighted China's intransigence, which in turn caused Washington to doubt its first line of defence.

Another characteristic of the military security dilemma between China and the United States is the fact that the difference between defensive and offensive realism has blurred. China's strategising is essentially defensive. Thus far it has been a conservative, security-seeking actor, aiming to protect its economic infrastructure along the coast and guard territorial sovereignty. But whereas its strategic objectives tend to be defensive, its tactical means to achieve them have become more and more offensive: long-range anti-ship missiles, attack submarines, and eventually probably intermediate-range manoeuvrable ballistic missiles and new surface combatants. The same is true for the United States. In signalling its resolve as an offshore balancer or to guard its first line of defence, it is using provocative tactics that range from sending civilian unarmed surveillance ships into areas claimed by the Chinese as EEZs, to positioning several aircraft carriers in China's vicinity. Pursuing an offensive defence may well result in cycles of ever-increasing brinkmanship spiralling out of control, as states try to prove the credibility of their threats. Moreover, Washington will continue to struggle with uncertainty about the nature and tenability of China's strategic self-restraint. That China has sought to limit its military modernisation during a period of rapid economic expansion and growing diplomatic assertive-ness may have as much to do with cautious planning to get the most advanced technologies possible and the aim to skip a generation of systems, as with deep-seated concerns about Washington's reactions. After all, Chinese decision-makers have made it clear time and again that America will have to learn to live with any increase in China's military power-projection capacity. It also remains to be seen how China will use its future capabilities to back its globalising economic inter-ests. Beijing has expressed its willingness to safeguard its stakes abroad, and although it is plausible that it will try to keep the costs low, there are no guarantees that it will stick to its tradi-tional non-interference policy or work with the United States to jointly tackle non-traditional security threats. This concern will probably add to America's distrust about China's future intentions.

A second conclusion is that the distinction between maritime and continental power is starting to blur. Optimists in the policy and academic community have contended that because of the geopolitical outlook of the Asia-Pacific, the two powers simply have no interest in encroaching on each other's spheres of influence. Boston University Professor Robert Ross, for example, has argued that America has no interest in trying to project its military might into the Asian hinterland, whereas China's vast continental frontier does not allow it to place strategic priority on maritime power.[123] Taylor Fravel put it thus: 'China's strategic goals are keyed to the defence of a continental power with growing maritime interests as well as to Taiwan's unification and are largely conservative, not expansionist. China is developing internal control, peripheral denial, and limited force-projection capabilities consistent with these objectives.'[124] Yet, oceans do not isolate. Tides of power in international history have rippled across the world's maritime spaces, in search of land or to quell enemies. When two powers on different continents vie for supremacy, the most effective option has always been to sow discord between the rival and its neighbours, but the most decisive has been the extent of control over their maritime interface.[125] Such maritime contests proved to be compelling zero-sum games. Extending defensive perimeters conceived by one power were a matter of naval expansionism in the eyes of the other. As early as 1942, the 'godfather of containment' Nicholas Spykman cautioned US strategists:

> A modern, vitalized, and militarized China is going to be a threat not only to Japan, but also to the position of the Western powers in the Asian Mediterranean. China will be a continental power of huge dimensions in control of a large section of the littoral of that middle sea.[126]

China's enhanced ability to defend its territorial interests in its littoral waters is seen by Washington as the erosion of its first line of defence. That China might soon commence developing weapons that threaten bases in Okinawa and Guam is seen as a serious threat to its second line of defence. But if it were to become a challenger with a large blue-water navy, the United States would probably view this as the beginning of a challenge in the western Pacific. Once China is able to decisively alter the naval balance in the Pacific, it could set sail for the waters south of the Eurasian continent. However many dialogues there are between both sides, and whatever the official discourses on a common interest in securing maritime commons, the driver of interaction between China and the US in the Pacific will remain an incessant quest to counterbalance each other's maritime power.

CHAPTER THREE

The Asian Response

While China's military modernisation has mainly developed in response to the superiority of the United States, the regional powers in Asia are closely watching how the altering balance of power between the two juggernauts could affect their strategic interests. Australia, India, Japan, Russia, ROK and Vietnam are obviously no mere spectators of the power plays between Washington and Beijing. Consider, for example, India's role as an emerging naval power presiding over the Indian Ocean, Japan as the geopolitical gatekeeper between continental Asia and the Pacific Ocean, or Vietnam, with its strategically located ports near to the South China Sea. Holding various geopolitical and military trump cards, these countries are particularly important as mediators of the Sino-American contest. Should Beijing manage to keep on good terms with them, it could also be more confident in demanding that the United States respect perceived core interests. Growing suspicion of China's military rise on their part might drive these protagonists closer to the US and prompt them to boost their own military capabilities. In the latter case, China's eventual progress in countering American preponderance will compromise Beijing's efforts to build stable relations with the rest of Asia. The ultimate outcome could be a dilemma between living with America's military hegemony and standing up against the entire neighbourhood.

The extent to which the other regional powers perceive China's military modernisation as a threat to their borders or maritime peripheries will be crucial in determining the course of regional politics. An important determinant in this regard is the extent to which they consider the PLA's military build-up as offensive. Historical legacies, differences in political identities and recent encounters with the PLA will also have played their part in informing these countries' perceptions.[1] Views of China's military power may have affected defence planning and the modernisation of capabilities in these states, prompting them to adopt strategies such as internal balancing, external balancing, hedging and bandwagoning. Internal balancing requires that a substantial part of a country's military means be exclusively committed to one specific threat and that it seeks to balance its rival independently. External balancing implies the formation of an alliance to counter an emerging threat. In hedging strategies, military build-ups can take place, but without assigning new capabilities to one particular challenger. Bandwagoning, or working with the emerging power, mostly occurs when a weaker state believes that the cost of countering a stronger power exceeds the benefits.

Japan

An authoritative report commissioned by the Ministry of Defense in 2009, warned that Japan's military power would soon be overshadowed by China's. Most decision-makers and opinion leaders have not ruled out that China *could* become a responsible power and maintain order in a way that is conducive to Japan's security interests. Yet, the mainstream thinking has been that this cannot be taken for granted. The lack of transparency of the PLA's rejuvenation and its provocative operations close to Japan's EEZ are considered signals that China's military intentions are not benign. The growing military power of China is seen in the context of lingering bilateral frictions over the East China Sea, over access to strategic sea lanes, the future of the Korean Peninsula, influence in Southeast Asia and the status of Taiwan on East Asia's strategic chessboard.[2]

Japan's distrust about China's intentions has grown.[3] Pointing to an expectation that Beijing would continue to convert its expanding economic resources into more robust military prowess, Japan's 2008 Defence White Paper stated: 'Japan is apprehensive about how the military power of China will influence the regional state of affairs and the security of Japan'.[4] The 2009 paper concentrated on China's regional power-projection capabilities and stressed that 'China began to work on acquiring capabilities for missions other than the Taiwan issue.' Assessing its impact on Japan's security, the paper referred to the increased presence of the Chinese Navy in the waters surrounding Japan. It referred to an incident in October 2008, when four Chinese naval vessels, including a *Sovremenny*-class destroyer, passed through the Tsugaru Strait to advance to the Pacific Ocean. This was the first identified passage by Chinese surface combatants through the strait to take a route circling Japan. In November 2008, four naval vessels, including a top-of-the-line *Luzhou*-class destroyer, passed between Okinawa Island and Miyako Island and headed to the Pacific Ocean. In December 2008, two Chinese maritime surveillance ships conducted navigation operations not permitted to foreign ships under international law, such as hovering and cruising within the territorial waters of Japan near the Senkaku/Diaoyu islands.[5] In March 2010, a flotilla of the North Sea Fleet sailed through the Miyako Strait on its way to the South China Sea. A month later, the Japanese Ministry of Defense reported three incidents of

PLAN helicopters approaching Japanese destroyers deployed to within 100m of Okinawa. Destroyers, frigates and submarines from the East Sea Fleet passed once more through Japan's Miyako Strait without notifying Tokyo and conducted anti-submarine warfare exercises in the Pacific southeast of Japan. A leading Japanese commentator had already warned of the possible consequences of such actions: 'China believes that its borders are not fixed. As the national general power, which consists of military power, political power, economic power and will of its people, gets stronger and stronger, its borders will tend to expand more outward.'[6]

The Japanese Defense Ministry has frequently accused China of developing weapons systems that go beyond defensive objectives; it has also conveyed its belief that this development raises doubts about China's peaceful intentions regard to the East China Sea and Taiwan. Various incidents with Chinese ships and aircraft in the waters around Taiwan have added to this fear. The PEW Research Center registered a steady deterioration between 2002 and 2008 in Japanese public opinion towards China. In 2008, about 84% of its respondents had a negative view of the country.[7] In 2009, a study of the Chicago Council showed that as much as 79% of Japanese people it spoke to predicted a China–Japan arms race if the US were to retreat.[8] This growing concern has triggered an intense debate about how Japan should deal with its neighbour's military ambitions, with the options considered ranging from Samuel Huntington's suggestion to strike a good bargain with Beijing to former Liberal Democratic Party (LDP) leader Ichiro Ozawa's proposal to 'make several thousands of warheads'[9].

The mainstream response has been to militarily balance China, but at the same time to avoid a spiralling effect by increasing military exchanges. Japan has a strong tendency to prevent confrontation and to adopt wait-and-see-pragmatism. 'Japan has shifted away from the friendship–diplomacy paradigm to a mixed strategy that involves both positive engagement and realistic balancing to hedge against the potential threats that China may pose in the future,' George Washington University's Mike Mochizuki said.[10] This has led Tokyo to stress the peaceful character of the modernisation of its Self Defense Forces. It explained that this rejuvenation is aimed not at China, but at a large number of traditional and non-traditional threats in Asia and beyond. Japan also sought to enhance its military interaction with China.[11] In 2006, the two sides started a bilateral security dialogue. The year after, Premier Yasuo Fukuda and his Chinese counterpart agreed to step up exchanges between military officers and defence universities. A Chinese warship ported for the first time in Japan and Japanese officers were invited to observe China's *Warrior 2007* manoeuvres.[12] In November 2009, the defence ministers of both countries agreed to organise joint exercises, to coordinate in UN peacekeeping operations, to work together in disaster relief and to develop a military maritime communication system.[13]

In spite of the increasing communication, Japan continued to lament Beijing's lack of transparency. It responded to the PLA's muscle flexing in the East China Sea with enhanced patrolling and an increasing number of interceptions of Chinese military aircraft. The modest outcomes of positive engagement with China have added impetus to military balancing policies. 'Preparation for full-scale aggression is essential,' the Ministry of Defense stressed in 2008. While the Democratic People's Republic of Korea is the greatest imminent threat, China figures as the most daunting security challenge for the future.[14] Japan's preparations for major armed contingencies entail preventing the enemy from acquiring air superiority, exhausting its capacity at sea, denying the access of landing operations at remote islands, cutting off maritime logistical support lines and defending Japan's maritime trade.[15] Therefore, Japan has invested in the development of various major conventional arms systems. In 2009, the Japan Maritime Self-Defense Force (JMSDF) commissioned its first of three new *Hyūga*-class helicopter carriers.[16] The largest Japanese warship since the Second World War, the *Hyūga* is Japan's answer to eventual denial operations by Chinese submarines.[17] By 2015, Japan will have four new 19DD-class destroyers, whose main task will be to patrol Japan's sea lanes and to defend its fleet against air attacks, alongside five new conventional *Sōryū*-class submarines and new P-X long-range maritime surveillance aircraft. Under the F-X programme, Japan is also seeking to replace its F-4 fighters by 2020, probably with the more potent Joint Strike Fighter. In addition, the Ministry of Defense is continuing to support the indigenous development of a Japanese stealth fighter, the *Shinshin*.[18]

While it does not enjoy the continental strategic depth of the other Asian powers, Japan's territory allows the dispersion of bases over a 3,000km-long chain of islands near to important sea lanes. Japan's facilities are more or less equally divided among three regional air defence commands, four escort flotillas and five armies. These have always been oriented towards two potential battlefields. The units in the north have evolved in readiness for a potential clash on the Korean Peninsula or contingencies with Russia. The southern units are mainly geared towards China and Taiwan. The Japanese Defense Forces are increasingly trained for rapid inter-regional deployment. In 2005, the Defense Agency approved a plan to defend the southern islands against an invasion, which included the rapid deployment of 55,000 troops drawn from the different armies, as well as planes, warships, and submarines from the air and maritime commands.[19] To this end, Japan has decided to develop a new central command and control system (CCS) that coordinates operations across regions and forces.[20] There have been several indications that Tokyo is concentrating specific capabilities to the south. Since 2006, Japan has been modernising its maritime-surveillance installations on the southern islands Kume, Miyako and Okinoerabu. In 2007, advanced P-3C maritime patrol aircraft were stationed in Naha and Kanoya, and a year later the F-4 fighters of this air force base were replaced with more advanced F-15 planes.[21] In 2009, the Defense Ministry announced its intention to permanently deploy troops on Yonaguni, one of Japan's southernmost islands, a stone's throw from Taiwan and the disputed Senkaku/Diaoyu islands.[22] In November 2010, the decision was finally made to base around 100 Ground Self-Defense Force troops on Yonaguni Island to monitor the coast and the activity of Chinese ships. Furthermore, the Ministry also expressed its interest to station troops on the Ishigaki and Miyako islands.[23]

The Kantei is thus making preparations for *internal* balancing strategies in response to China's military rise. This could partly result from concerns that its alliance with the US may not offer the assurance it once did, despite public statements to the contrary. Both sides have more overtly emphasised the relevance of the alliance vis-à-vis China.[24] The 2005 statement of the US–Japan Security Consultative Committee caused frustration in Beijing because it listed the 'peaceful resolution of issues concerning the Taiwan Strait' and 'encouraging China to improve transparency in its military affairs' as joint objectives.[25] The Japanese Defense Ministry also considers enhancing the integration of tactical command-and-control structures as an insurance that the US will live up to its commitments. Defence officials on both sides of the Pacific referred to budgetary constraints to support their pledge for tighter alliances and burden sharing. Yet, a certain wariness remains. Japan has always feared being left behind in Washington's strategising and worried that the US would not risk Los Angeles for Tokyo, as was the case during the Cold War.[26] China's growing military power has rekindled this apprehension.[27] Some Japanese spectators have expressed their frustration about America's reluctance to formally extend its defence cooperation to the disputed East China Sea.[28] After China's naval posturing and the collision between Japanses Coast Guard vessels and a Chinese trawler in 2010, Japanese analysts similarly complained that the US offered little support. Others lamented the depletion of US military presence in the region because of the wars in Iraq and Afghanistan, at a time when Washington was passing the bill for relocating its marines to Guam to Japanese taxpayers.[29] Hardliners argue that preventive strikes should be considered against the growing threat of North Korean and Chinese missiles, though they know Washington would never accept this course of action.[30] Finally, for many Japanese, US policy towards Beijing has been too accommodating. These critics see a weakened superpower putting more effort into close relations with China than with its ally Japan.[31] This has not really changed with the various incidents in 2010. Indeed, China's assertiveness has prompted the Japanese to call on Washington to show its resolve. During the 2010 Asia-Pacific Economic Cooperation (APEC) summit, Prime Minister Naoto Kan even stated: 'I'd like to point out that in Japan and in other nations in the region, people, including myself, have renewed our understanding that the presence of the US and the presence of the US military are becoming increasingly important to maintain peace and stability in the region.'[32] But for all the eagerness to strengthen security cooperation, doubts remain over why the US has shown so much restraint and politely taken China's grievances into account when deciding to stage a large exercise with the ROK in the Sea of Japan instead of the Yellow Sea. Aside from this exercise, which the countries undertook in response to the March 2010 sinking of the South Korean corvette *Cheonan*, allegedly by a North Korean torpedo, the US has hardly recip-rocated China's growing naval activity.

India

India too has increased its efforts to counter China, while simul-taneously enhancing its military-to-military relations with the PRC.[33] Ever since the Indo-Chinese War of 1962, the Indian armed forces have been vigilant in guarding the continental borders. Since China started prioritising its naval power, the Indian mili-tary has also expressed concern about a future encroachment on its maritime sphere of influence. Against the background of deepening economic and political relations, the official discourse on China's threat has been volatile. After the *Pokhran II* crisis in 1998, when India tested a nuclear weapon and stated that this was aimed at China, the official line became more conciliatory. Both Bharatiya Janata Party (BJP) and Congress administrations have downplayed the China threat. In 2008 Premier Manmohan Singh even proclaimed his plan to turn the border area into 'mountains of peace'. In 2003, Delhi and Beijing agreed on new confidence-building measures, resulting in the first port call by six Indian ships from the Eastern Naval Command and a joint maritime search-and-rescue exercise. In 2006, a memorandum of understanding was signed that envisaged regular institu-tional contacts between armed forces and defence officials. The year after, Indian armies joined a military exercise on land in China's Yunnan Province. In 2008, 137 Chinese soldiers partici-pated in a large nine-day training manoeuvre in India.

This rapprochement notwithstanding, public perceptions of China did not improve. Between 2002 and 2007, the percentage of Indians who viewed the PRC's ascent as negative increased from 22 to 64. Political and military leaders remained hostile as well. In the parliament, the Congress-led administration was repeatedly attacked for wheedling China at the expense of national security. Navy Chief Sureesh Mehta publicly derided the China threat thesis, but also pointed out that India was surrounded by countries that are inclined towards China and that they could turn against India.[34] Vice-Admiral Raman Suthan, Commander of the Eastern Fleet, claimed during a 2007 visit to a Kolkata dockyard that:

> China has fuel interests of its own as fuel lines from Africa and the Gulf run through these waters, and so they are also building up their Navy. The naval fleet in east India has long legs and, with the government's emphasis on the 'look east' policy, we are strengthening the east now.

In 2009, Air Chief Marshal Fali Homi Major asserted that: 'China is a totally different ballgame compared to Pakistan … We know very little about the actual capabilities of China, their combat edge or how professional their military is … they are certainly a greater threat.'[35] Apart from the fierce reactions to alleged incursions by small Chinese military units along the disputed border, New Delhi has received the deployment of PLAN ships in the Gulf of Aden with suspicion. In 2009, military tensions along the border culminated in the cancellation of a planned exercise. Highlighting this uncertainty, National Security Adviser M.K. Narayanan said: 'What we really need is a broad national consensus on whether China is a threat, or a neighbour we can go along with. We also need consensus on the possible terms of a border solution.'

Since the late 1990s, the dominant view among Indian defence experts was that China, consolidating its supremacy in the Taiwan Strait, would reach out to the rest of Asia. According to T.D. Joseph, Senior Fellow at the Center for Air Power Studies:

Even though it is argued that China's military build-up is intended to deter the US capabilities of support-ing Taiwan and to coerce the latter into reunification, the capabilities that it is acquiring and is planning to acquire are far in excess of those required for such an effort. With China planning to acquire more long range nuclear submarines, aircraft carriers, AWACS [airborne warning and control systems], long range bombers, effective aerial refuelling capability and fifth generation combat aircraft in numbers several times those of India, the balance would definitely shift in favour of China in the future.[36]

Jagannath Panda, of the Institute for Defence Studies and Security Analyses (IDSA), believes China is boosting its military diplomacy to build a secure neighbourhood before gradually extending its influence throughout the world.[37] In the same vein East Asia specialist Sujit Dutta sees potential disputes arising from competition for dominance within the Indian Ocean:

China's military modernisation will affect India whether we like it or not, especially when the bound-ary issue is not settled. A permanent Chinese naval presence in the Indian Ocean would be a red line for India. If China's navy comes into this area and says 'we are going to protect our trade', then that changes the whole game.[38]

India is suspicious too of Washington's stance on Chinese military modernisation. Brahma Chellaney of India's Centre for Policy Research pointed out that Washington has turned down Taiwan's request to purchase diesel-powered submarines and attack helicopters, welcomed China's deployment of warships in the Gulf of Aden and left India alone in the fight against Pakistani-fomented transnational terror. He writes: 'As a financially strapped US, mired in two wars, builds a stronger cooperative relationship with China out of necessity, strains in its existing alliances in Asia will surface.'[39] Various other experts have endorsed this analysis that India should not rely on America to defend its security interests, and that New Delhi needed to aim at an independent strategy to dissuade Beijing from further strengthening its military presence in South Asia.

Taking changes in its military modernisation as another variable for deducing its security objectives, India has unmistakably set the ambition to consolidate its military presence from the Himalayas to Antarctica and from the Strait of Hormuz to the Andaman Sea. Since 2002, it has replaced its Pakistan-centric posture with more ambitious positioning across the South Asian region. Onshore, it has modernised its bases in the northeast. After increased activity by small Chinese units at the end of 2007, the minister of defence, the national security adviser, and the chiefs of the Eastern and Northern Command agreed to step up the army's strength in Assam and Arunashal Pradesh. In December 2007, the 27th Division from the 33rd Corps was relocated to its home base in Kalimpong, near the strategically important tri-junction between Bhutan, China and India, after being deployed for more than ten years in Kashmir. The minister also approved plans to revamp the 4th Corps based in Tezpur and the 2nd Corps based in Dimapur. Senior officers announced more sophisticated weapons with a range of up to 100km or more would be deployed in his area. '105mm field guns and howitzers and 155mm *Bofors* howitzers are already deployed on the border', a senior officer pointed out, 'together with facilities like laser and radar jamming systems. These guns can penetrate up to 30km inside China.'[40] To improve mobility along the border, the Ministry of Defence approved the construction of a new network of roads and railways. The Indian Air Force followed this trend. The strengthening of the Eastern Air Command's capacity has been impressive. The Indian government decided to base squadrons of its most potent fighter jets, the Su-30MKI, in the eastern Sector from 2008 onwards. The first two squadrons with 36 fighters were stationed at Tezpur airbase.[41] Apart from the *Sukhoi*, Tezpur will be strengthened with new air-defence systems and advanced combat helicopters that are better equipped for high-altitude warfare and lifting of advanced landing groups. In addition to Tezpur, the Indian Air Force is in the process of upgrading its other airbases in the eastern sector. The length of runway at the base in Kalaikunda in West Bengal state has been extended to support forward operations in Arunachal.[42] The command has also refurbished its forward airbases at Chabua, Jorhat and Hash Mara air bases. In 2009, Indian news media reported that the Indian government would create two new divisions and an artillery brigade near to the Chinese border.[43]

After consolidating its naval presence in the Arabian Gulf by constructing a new navy base in Kadamba, New Delhi has announced plans to build an even larger base for the Eastern Naval Command in Rambilli near to Vizag, which will harbour three new P-17 *Shivalik*-class frigates, P-28 anti-submarine warfare corvettes, P-75 *Scorpène* submarines, P8I *Orion* long-range maritime reconnaissance aircraft and the new *INS Vikramaditya* aircraft carrier.[44] Since the tsunami of 2004 devastated large parts of the facilities at Port Blair in the Andaman Sea, Indian defence commentators have been discussing how to fully exploit the strategic location of this maritime stronghold. In 2005 military installations were repaired and new radar systems were reportedly installed.[45] Because of the unpredictable weather conditions, the Indian government has been reluctant to dispatch more military aircraft permanently at Nicobar airport, but it has increased the number of aerial manoeuvres around the island. In October 2010, the wing commander of Nicobar Island announced that by 2010, his base would have fully fledged flight detachment, an advanced radar system and an air defence weapons squadron. India has thus made significant steps in shifting its naval power from the western part of the Indian Ocean to the east. If it manages to dominate the strategic sea lanes between Southeast Asia and the Middle East, this will certainly become a formidable source of conventional deterrence against China.

In April 2007, India successfully tested its *Agni*-III intermediate-range ballistic missile (IRBM). This missile was designed to reach China. India's previous ballistic missiles, the *Agni*-I and -II had a rather short-action radius and were mainly developed to deter Pakistan. The *Agni*-III is India's first missile that could reach deep into China's territory, and the PRC is also the only nuclear power that would be a relevant target within its 3,500km to 4,000km range. Although New Delhi stated that this vehicle would not be equipped with nuclear warheads, the missile supports a wide range of warhead configurations with a total payload ranging from 600kg to 1,800kg. Moreover, the Defence Research and Development Organisation (DRDO), the main agency charged with the development of India's nuclear arsenal, is reportedly working on MIRV technology to enable the *Agni*-III to circumvent Chinese missile defence countermeasures. The fact that the construction of this missile type was ordered in 2001, at a time when ties with Beijing were improving, in combination with mounting development costs, demonstrates that nuclear deterrence is still central to India's China agenda.

Of all Asian powers, India is the one that has most visibly sought to respond to China's military rise by internal balancing. The construction of new bases near the Chinese border, the expansion of naval capabilities along the sea lanes in the Gulf of Bengal, and the development of new intermediate-range missiles show the shifting strategic attention from Pakistan to India's eastern security frontier.

Russia

Russia has historically been less worried about a Chinese military threat because the long buffer of tundra and mountains protects its main urban and industrial centres in the west. Recently, however, it has come to realise that the military balance is altering in China's favour, in a large part thanks to Russian arms exports.[46] In a major volume on Russia's security environment, two senior military officers said: 'China now has the superiority in conventional arms and military equipment compared to Russia, and that it will reach parity with the US by 2015.'[47] Yet, this modernisation has seldom been linked to bilateral tensions. China, for example, has been widely accused of pulling the Russian Far East into its economic orbit, but Moscow has maintained that as long as the Chinese merchants and migrants pay their taxes, there would not be a security problem.[48] Moreover, decision-makers in Moscow have increasingly recognised that the stability of the Far East would depend on new linkages with Chinese industry.[49] China has also been touted as a future challenger of Russia's interests in Central Asia, but this has not caused widespread concern about potential military ambitions. Alexander Kadyrbaev of the Russian Academy of Sciences contended that in spite of its increasing commercial influence, China would not be able to challenge Russia's position in Central Asia. Local people, he said, had a traditional distrust of outsiders, and with the US military knocking on its back door, Beijing now had a strong interest in working with Moscow.[50] Ajdar Kurtov, of the Russian Institute for Strategic Studies, has said that even when China obtained access to the region's natural resources and exported its goods, this would still contribute to Russia's interest in stabilising Central Asia.[51] Other experts have stressed China's soaring need for energy and safe shipping lanes to the Arctic Ocean. As Russia's interest in exploiting resources and controlling sea lanes grew, Russian officials took the view that the Arctic, if properly managed, could enhance Moscow's strategic leverage.[52] Russia has thus recognised its neighbour's growing influence in Asia, but there is no great concern that Beijing will use its military might to defend and extend its interests.[53] This confidence was reflected in the 2009 National Security Strategy. The Russian Security Council mentioned China only once – as one its allies in what is known as the 'BRIC' grouping of Brazil, Russia, India and China – which was in marked contrast to the significant attention spent on NATO and the US.[54] The only security threat in East Asia that the Council mentioned in the strategy was an eventual conflict on the Korean Peninsula. With regard to new provisions to maintain security along the border, the focus was on Ukraine, the Caucasus and Central Asia, rather than the Far East.[55]

A first explanation for Russia being less worried about China as a potential military challenger is that, apart from armed skirmishes on the border in 1969, it has no history of major historical armed conflicts with China. The military elite has continued to concentrate on the alleged military encroachment of the West, notably NATO's enlargement to the east, and America's military cooperation with the Caucasus and Central Asia. China's modernising armed forces are ranked much lower as a threat than the security policies of the West. Moreover, various observers in Moscow have welcomed this evolution as it provides new options for opposing the US. Defence ministers Sergey Ivanov and Anatoliy Serdyukov have been staunch adherents of the new kind of Eurasianism, which seeks to strengthen Russia's geopolitical position as the continental centre between Asia and Europe, to counterbalance the West by building new alliances in the East and to appreciate similarities in the political systems of developmentalist Asian countries as an alternative to Western liberalism. For this reason they both invested heavily in new military synergies with Beijing. During their tenures, both men actively lobbied their Chinese counterparts to stage large-scale joint exercises, accompanied by staunch anti-American rhetoric on the Russian side. Various experts have defended this view. Colonel-General Leonid Ivashov, Vice-President of the Academy of Geopolitical Problems, posited that China's modernising defence apparatus would help shape a stronger alliance of countries that do not agree with the existing world order.[56] Andrei Kokoshin, Dean of the Faculty of World Politics of Moscow State University, suggested the military strength of a Russia–India–China triangular alliance may offset US dominance.[57] Yevgeny Bazhanov, Vice-Rector of the Diplomatic Academy of the Ministry of Foreign Affairs, argued:

> China has consistently sought to strengthen ties with Russia in the military, political, economic and humanitarian spheres. It is not building up military assets close to Russian borders, does not enter into any anti-Russian coalition, shares the negative attitude of Moscow to the enlargement of NATO, works with Russia in the Shanghai Cooperation Organization, and is actively engaged with our country in the UN.[58]

Military Academy Director Mahmut Gareev conceded that 'many powers desire to make a quantum leap in achieving military-technological superiority and to build up their presence near to Russia,' but he concluded that China's posture was cooperative.[59] If China's military transition has already appeared on Russia's radar screen, it is still seen as less threatening than the US presence in Eurasia. Russia has, therefore, more interest in aligning with the PRC. For Moscow, the main military challenge in Asia is to prepare for an eventual clash between China and a US-centred coalition.

Yet, while Eurasian optimism rapidly gained ground in the decade after Boris Yeltsin's charm offensive to the West, and Sino-Russian military exchanges visibly expanded, experts started to criticise the Kremlin for being too lenient with China. Andrei Piontkovsky, Executive Director of the Strategic Studies Center in Moscow, wrote:

> The Kremlin was short-sighted in hunting the 'phantom of the American threat'. China will never be interested in the economic and political modernisation of Russia, because he prefers that Russia remains a source of mineral and energy resources, as well as a strategic rear in its troublesome relations with the United States. Similarly, the Shanghai Cooperation Organization, in the eyes of China is an instrument of regional policy that helps strengthen China's influence and control over natural resources in Central Asia at the expense of Russia.[60]

Others take a less relaxed view of Russian accommodation. Konstantin Sivkov, a member of the Strategic Studies Center of the General Staff, said that thus far China had only been deterred by its dependence on oil and Russia's nuclear supremacy, but that if Russia further weakened and fragmented, China might want to claim a part of Russian territory and resources, invade and occupy the far-eastern region of Primorskiy Krai and seek to protect Chinese citizens.[61] Alexander Hramchihin, of the independent Institute of Political and Military Analyses, has scorned Moscow's failure to keep its military capabilities in the Far East on a par with China's. For the longer term, this represented an invitation for Beijing to turn this region into its back yard, he warns.[62] For news commentator Artur Blinov, Moscow has yet to formulate its strategy towards China, although it is aware of 'broad interests in the Far East' that a rising China could threaten.[63]

Since the end of the Cold War, the advanced units of Russia's armed forces have systematically been designated to the Caucasus Military District and the major urban and industrial areas. Tumbling defence budgets, a lack of political interest and awkward logistics have rendered units in Siberia and the Far East prone to the severe depletion of human resources and technological backwardness. Due to insufficient maintenance, the Pacific Fleet degraded into a floating junkyard, and the air force only managed to conserve a few of its obsolete fighters by selling fuel and spare parts.[64] President Vladmir Putin was the first to recognise the embarrassing state of the army in the Far Eastern and Siberian Military District. In 2004 and 2007, Putin visited the Kamchatka Naval Base and stated that the modernisation of the Pacific Fleet would be a priority. Since then the Russian Navy has invested in improving the naval ports in the Northern Territories (Kuril Islands), Vladivostok and Kamchatka. Most of these projects were related to improving the basic living conditions, rather than modernising combat systems. A major step, however, was the announcement to invest $300m in a new atomic submarine base in Vilyuchinsk, Kamchatka, to be the first homeport the future *Borei* strategic missile submarine.[65] In October 2010, the Ministry of Defence announced that all piers and facilities of the Vilyuchinsk base had been refurbished, new security and communications systems had been introduced, and that the training centre was modernised.

With regard to the allocation of other future navy ships like the *Gorshkov* frigate, the *Slava* nuclear attack submarine and the future generation aircraft carrier, the Pacific Fleet seems to be catching up with its northern counterpart that used to be more privileged in the commissioning of new vessels.[66] The Far East Integrated Air Force in Novosibirsk was the first to receive 24 upgraded Su-24 M2 jet fighters. The Ministry of Defence announced that by 2012 the Su-24s were to be replaced by the Su-34 fighter-bomber. That year, the 23rd Fighter Aviation Wing in Khabarovsk and the 22nd Wing in Primorskiy Krai received the improved Su-27SM fighter.[67] Pilots in these units also saw a significant increase in their flight hours, and the merging of air force and Air Defence into one joint command is expected to lead to more effective C4I2.[68] Both the Siberian and Far Eastern Military Districts were furnished with new Type 90S main battle tanks. In the 2010 *Vostok* exercise, Russia for the first time mobilised its armed forces in the Far East for simulating an armed conflict with a neighbouring country. In contrast to previous manoeuvres, which were smaller and mainly focussed on non-traditional security threats, its Pacific Fleet was supported by vessels from other fleets to stage a large-scale anti-submarine warfare drill. The newly established Joint Air Defence Command conducted a live-fire exercise with its new S-300 missile batteries. Yet, it is too early to conclude that this evolution signals the Kremlin's intention to respond to China's military prowess. Most of these new projects were just modest steps in the direction of normalisation. The systems that Moscow is replacing are among the oldest in the entire region and the units in the Far East are primarily tasked with guarding the unstable Korean Peninsula and the disputed islands the Sea of Okhotsk, as well as showing the Russian flag as far afield as the eastern Pacific and the Indian Ocean.[69]

The three main regional powers – India, Japan and Russia – are thus increasingly investing in the modernisation of their armed forces. This effort is guided by multi-direction security strategies that take a wide range of threats into account. The rapid proliferation of terrorism and other non-traditional threats have certainly drawn more attention in these countries' strategising. The fact that a large part of their defence budgets is still allocated to new military systems such as submarines, destroyers, fighter-bomber jets, main battle tanks and air-defence systems, however, shows that the scenario of interstate warfare has not been ruled out. The assumption that such purchases might have been motivated by the wish to bolster domestic industries is not valid, because Japan and India relied on expensive imported equipment and the Russian government started to restructure its defence industries so that their productivity is boosted often at the expense of employment and profit. Neither is it just a matter of path dependence or a natural cycle of replacing ageing weapons: all the major powers have introduced various new types of armament. Nationalism – another factor invoked to explain military spending – is equally insufficient as an explanation. Despite the eagerness to identify national status with the success of economic growth, military power has remained an important tool for political elites to muster domestic and international prestige. The military normalisation of Japan is an obvious example, as is the propaganda that coincided with the announcement to build aircraft carriers in China. Yet, many important systems like tactical ballistic missiles and submarines were launched quietly or even secretly. Military modernisation stems thus mainly from conventional threat perceptions.

Australia

Australian authorities do not fear a direct confrontation with China. An obvious reason is a maritime buffer of more than 4,000km. 'We are distant from traditional theatres of conflict between the major powers, and there is an absence of any serious, enduring disputes with our neighbours that could provide a motive for an attack,' the Australian Department of Defence said in 2009.[70] Sino-Australian relations are untainted by a history of rivalry, nor is there competition for regional leadership. 'Australia understands that it is playing in a different league,' an Australian official stated.[71] Under prime ministers John Howard and Kevin Rudd, Australia avoided public allusions to Chinese military challenges and consistently highlighted maturing economic linkages as the best antidote to conflict. In 2005, the Australian Defence Minister said he saw China's expanding military expenditure as a process of modernisation, not destabilisation. A poll conducted by the Lowy Institute in 2008 suggested that 60% of Australians thought that China's aim was to dominate Asia, but as a security threat it was ranked below many non-traditional threats.[72] In keeping with these findings, Australia staged its first live-firing naval exercise with China in September 2010. At the time, an Australian navy officer told the press: 'there is nothing more effective than working closely together in a military exercise to build trust and friendship between Navies and nations'.[73]

Yet, Australia is concerned it could be drawn in as a third party in an eventual stand-off in the Taiwan Strait or a major conflict between the PRC and Japan or the US. 'With China's growth will come increasing competition with the United States for strategic influence,' the Ministry of Defence explained in its White Paper of 2005. 'This will shape future regional security arrangements as countries seek to balance the demands that will accrue from their relationships with [China and the United States].'[74] This was restated in the 2007 version.[75] The 2009 White Paper spoke of a remote but plausible potential for confrontation with a major-power adversary.[76] In this document the Defence Ministry said it expected China would become the strongest Asian military power by a considerable margin. It went on:

> [China's] military modernisation will be increasingly characterised by the development of power projection capabilities. A major power of China's stature can be expected to develop a globally significant military capability befitting its size. But the pace, scope and structure of China's military modernisation have the potential to give its neighbours cause for concern if not carefully explained.[77]

Another concern for Australia is that China's arms race with Taiwan could pave the way for a robust military presence in the South China Sea. 'Having resolved its immediate dilemma over the island [Taiwan],' James Holmes and Toshi Yoshihara stressed, 'China might employ its sea-denial strategy in the South China Sea, an area of vital interest to Australia.'[78] Similarly, Paul Dibb has claimed:

> The strong growth of China's political and military power will enable it to dominate its maritime approaches and make survival much more hazardous for US naval forces, especially in the Taiwan Strait. We can expect to see China have more influence even than today in Southeast Asia, which it sees as its natural sphere of influence, and it may come to have more influence in South Korea than the United States.[79]

Another scholar, Hugh White, went as far as claiming that China's rise may finally close the era of Western maritime domination of the Asian Pacific.[80] The Australian government has picked up these concerns about China's power, but discussions about its impact have been kept behind closed doors.

The Australian political elite has thus depicted itself as growing close to China, when in reality it was anxious that the country's rise could get out of control. The 2009 Defence White Paper was a first important step in translating these fears into defence-modernisation plans.[81] China was one of the focal points in this document, and even when it was not said explicitly, much of the new arms procurements aimed at 'forces that can exert air superiority and sea control in our approaches'. This blueprint of Australia's future armed forces can be interpreted as a plan to create a security perimeter against conventional threats:

> Depending on developments in the Asia-Pacific region over the next two decades, Australia might need to selectively project military power or demonstrate strategic presence beyond our primary operational environment. For example, this might occur in maritime Southeast Asia, should this be necessary to deter or defeat armed attacks on Australia, or protect our strategic interests in the wider Asia-Pacific region, in concert with allies and partners with whom we share similar strategic interests in meeting common security challenges.[82]

To fulfil this objective, the Australian government decided to increase defence spending by 3% each year, despite a climate of economic uncertainty. Large parts of the budget were allocated to major conventional arms systems. Besides 12 conventional submarines, the navy ordered three air warfare destroyers, eight frigates fit for hunting submarines, and naval surveillance aircraft. The air force announced the procurement of 100 F-35 Joint Strike Fighters, five KC-30A air-to-air refuelling aircraft and six new Airborne Early Warning and Control (AWACs) aircraft.

This build-up will result in a decisive alteration of the military balance with Australia's immediate rival, Indonesia. But the extended range of most systems, the advanced air-defence systems, and the remarkable leap forward in anti-submarine warfare capacities all show that this modernisation goes beyond the objective to prevail over potential Southeast Asian contenders. 'It is important for our own capability requirements for the Australian Defence Force to be prepared to meet a range of contingencies arising from military and naval build-ups across our region,' Prime Minister Rudd stated in May 2009. 'That is prudent, long-term defence planning, and we believe we've got the balance absolutely right.'[83]

Off the record, however, defence officials explain that the aim is to establish a maritime defence perimeter and to keep all options open to protect interests or to assist allies in major wars beyond the South Pacific. 'Even if we would not like to fight China, we might not have the choice to pick the fight, so we can better be prepared,' one senior military expert remarked.[84] The baseline has thus been strategic autonomy, which also applied to the United States. Indeed, the US has been a sort of life insurance, but, to borrow the words of an Australian official, 'the aim was to avoid costly accidents'. Australia, therefore, tended to be cautious of encouraging the US to stand strong in the East Asian littorals. As one senior diplomat suggested, 'the US might have to understand that [it] cannot take [the] current level of military presence in East Asia for granted.'[85]

The Republic of Korea

The ROK has often been portrayed as the Asian power that would be least inclined to respond negatively to China's modernising military power. Following on from the conciliatory policies of presidents Kim Dae-Jung and Roh Moo-hyun between 1998 and 2008, authors such as David Kang have claimed that strong historical and cultural linkages, in addition to growing commercial and interpersonal communication, would mitigate threat perceptions. 'Interactions between South Korea and China have been largely positive, from cooperation over the North Korean issue, to expanding economic and cultural ties between the South and China,' Kang argued.[86] Indeed, both Kim and Roh downplayed rumours about Chinese military domination in the region, highlighting the need to work with Beijing with regard to North Korea and actively promoted new military exchanges. In spite of this conciliatory posture, polls have shown that the majority of the population continued to see China as a military threat that will become a potential source of conflict between major powers in Asia.[87] Nearly 90% of South Koreans interviewed in a 2007 poll believed that the growth of Chinese military power would be a potential source of conflict between major powers in Asia.[88] A 2009 poll confirmed that 74% of South Koreans had negative views of China's military power and that 89% feared a China–Japan arms race, should the US retreat.[89] Annual surveys carried out by the Korean National Defence University between 1997 and 2004 have demonstrated that only 10% expected that China would take a friendly position towards Seoul in case of an armed conflict with the North, whereas 35% believed it would back Pyongyang.[90] Interdependence and China's assumed soft power in Northeast Asia have thus not neutralised insecurity about China's military intentions.

This undercurrent of popular distrust has come to the surface in assessments by defence planners, in expert writings and in the strategies of Roh's successor Lee Myung-bak.[91] The White Papers of the Defence Ministry have increasingly pointed at China's growing military capabilities. Whereas the 2000 edition merely touched upon this issue, the 2006 edition highlighted the growing ability to exert force beyond Taiwan. 'The army aims at moving from regional defence to trans-regional mobility,' it stated. 'The navy aims at a gradual extension of the strategic depth for offshore defence operations. The air force aims at having long-distance operation capabilities.'[92]

Civilian security experts have restated this assessment in various studies. There is growing concern that, rather than posing a direct threat, China's new capabilities could add to regional instability and may draw the ROK into wars with other regional powers. 'The Northeast Asia region, surrounding the Korean Peninsula is unstable,' Defence Minister Lee Sang-hee promulgated at the 2009 IISS Shangri-La Dialogue. 'While interdependency among nations ha[s] increased through greater economic cooperation and exchange, there are still many potential causes for conflict such as history recognition, territoriality, and competition for resources.'[93] In an unprecedented statement in Australia, President Lee warned that a 15% increase in China's military budget could influence the defensive strategies of other countries like Japan and South Korea. 'In Northeast Asia it is not desirable to have countries engaged in a race for military build-up, or increasing their military spending,' he said.[94]

China's soft approach towards the DPRK after the sinking of the *Cheonan* in 2010 was also widely considered as a tipping point in the relations between Seoul and Beijing. 'Before the *Cheonan*, the Sino-South Korean relationship had been on honeymoon,' one observer said. 'That is over now: the two countries will have to face uncomfortable truths from now on, including disputes surrounding the territory, American troops stationed in South Korea, and the Northeast Project, to name just a few.'[95] China refused to condemn North Korea, rejected the findings of an international report about the attack and waited a month to express condolences for the loss of 46 South Korean sailors. Yet, a survey carried out by Seoul National University's Institute for Peace and Unification Studies showed that the majority of South Koreans lacked confidence in the international report's conclusions that the sinking of the *Cheonan* was caused by a North Korean torpedo.[96] South Korean officials and experts explained that even though China did not publicly denounce the attack, it did make its concerns very clear during closed talks between Hu Jintao and Kim Jong-il in May 2010 and reportedly declined Kim's demand for economic and military assistance.[97] But, whereas China's diplomatic pragmatism might to some degree have been acceptable, China deeply disturbed South Korea by responding aggressively to the US–ROK military exercises that were organised in response to the sinking. Deputy Chief of Staff Ma Xiaotian declared that the PRC 'was very opposed' to the scheduled manoeuvres in the Yellow Sea.[98] Articles in government newspapers quoted Chinese experts saying that the exercises were a threat to China's core interests.[99] A few days before the US–ROK drill was due to start, the PLAN staged its own military exercise in the international waters of the Yellow Sea.

The main fear for the ROK is that China's military modernisation leads to a tit-for-tat game with Japan, probably aided by the US, and that this would leave Seoul between a rock and a hard place.[100] In the case of escalating military tensions between Beijing and Tokyo, it is assumed that Seoul will have to choose between working with Japan, with whom it has its own historical and territorial frictions, or with China. Should Seoul opt for the former, it could be punished by Beijing, which could use its growing military prowess to extend its control over the Korean Peninsula, if it were to attain military supremacy in the region.[101] A second scenario is that if an arms race between China, Japan and the US escalated into an armed conflict in the green waters around China, Washington would request access to South Korean facilities for operations against the PLA. This could again lead to retaliation.[102] Finally, there is the risk of confrontation with the Chinese armed forces, should the DPRK collapse. South Korean experts have emphasised that the ROK and China have a shared interest in stabilising their reclusive neighbour.[103] Seoul and Beijing have also often taken identical positions vis-à-vis Japan and the US in the Six-Party Talks. But this has not offset doubts about China's ultimate decisions, should the Kim dynasty collapse or should Pyongyang order an attack on the South.[104]

South Korea has one of the most rapidly growing defence budgets in Asia. In 2006, the government decided to more than double defence expenditures by 2015. About half of this increase, some $620bn, would be allocated to force modernisation in order to achieve the objective of 'self-reliant war deterrence' and 'cooperative self-reliant defence' by 2020.[105] It will be invested in, inter alia, new *Sejong* destroyers, each carrying 128 missiles guided by an advanced Aegis system, nine conventional submarines, 20 frigates for anti-submarine warfare purposes, three *Dokdo*-class landing platform docks and mine-countermeasure helicopters. Its air force will purchase F-15K *Slam Eagle* air-superiority fighters, four Boeing 737 AWAC aircraft and probably F-35 Joint Strike Fighters. Its land forces will receive 600 indigenously produced K2 *Black Panther* main battle tanks. Its air and missile defence capabilities will be expanded by purchasing additional *Patriot* and SM-2 missile batteries. Apart from dissuading a North Korean attack, the purpose of these new self-reliant defence and deterrence capabilities is to be able to engage in a wide range of regional armed contingencies, without having to counterbalance China by joining any alliance. In the words of one expert at the Korean National University: 'The essence of our military strategy towards China is to counterbalance it without letting it look like balancing.'[106]

Vietnam

Vietnam too has been combining confidence-building and balancing strategies. It has in the first place sought to prevent territorial disputes with China from spilling over into military rivalry. In 2006, it agreed with China to stage joint navy patrols in the Beibu Bay and to open a telephone hotline between the armed forces for avoiding military escalations at sea. Yet, Vietnamese decision-makers were increasingly disturbed that neither these frail synergies between armed forces nor the 2003 Code of Conduct on the South China Sea was leading Beijing to practise restraint. Moreover, since mid-2009, China has become more assertive in pushing its territorial claims. During a rare visit to an island midway between Vietnam and Hainan, President Nguyen Minh Triet stated that: 'We will not let anyone infringe on our territory. We will not make concessions, even an inch of ground to anyone.'

Responding to the capture of a Vietnamese fishing boat, Vice Admiral Nguyen Van Hien stressed that the Navy would protect Vietnamese fishermen against new Chinese aggression, leaving open the option that China's behaviour might still change in a positive way. In 2010, Vietnam unveiled an $8.5bn economic and defence development plan for a chain of islands along the coastline. At the same time Hanoi sought external support. It suggested using ASEAN as a platform for developing a new legally binding agreement for the South China Sea. But as Beijing managed to sow division among the ASEAN members, the Vietnamese government recognised the need for stronger partners.

Even though the 2009 Defence White Paper explicitly denounced new military alliances, Russia soon re-emerged as a privileged supporter. New contracts were signed for six *Kilo*-class submarines, 24 advanced *Su*-30MK2 maritime bombers and up to four *Gepard* frigates. Russia is also contracted to build a new naval base, maintenance facilities and a telecommunications centre, and to provide training for Vietnamese navy officers. With India, Hanoi increased the number of military dialogues and the frequency of joint manoeuvres. In 2005, military relations were re-established with the United States, leading to a memorandum on port calls and an annual strategic dialogue. In 2010, cooperation was lifted to a higher level with visits from *USS George Washington* and the *USS John McCain*, the first such visits in 35 years. The countries' defence ministries discussed cooperation in humanitarian assistance, search and rescue, international peacekeeping and maritime security. But whereas cooperation with the armed forces of Russia and India has not been questioned, expanding ties with Washington did meet a lot of internal criticism. 'While our political leaders fret about losing the country to China, they also fear [the consequences for] the Party's ideological leadership by getting close to America,' a Vietnamese scholar argued.[107] Suspicion of the United States remains strong and several analysts complained that the US Navy's presence in the South China Sea was a source of instability.

Conclusion

While the PLA is not seen as the most imminent threat, other Asian powers are anxious that China's growth could coincide with more assertive security policies across the region, and ultimately diminish restraint in using military force. For Japan, the immediate security priorities have been the conflict between the two Koreas and the continuing dispute with Russia over the Kuriles/Northern Territories. But as a consequence of China's growing naval power, Tokyo has come to doubt Beijing's benevolent intentions in the East China Sea. The commissioning of new destroyers, anti-submarine warfare capabilities, submarines and the refitting of facilities on its southernmost islands express this perceived insecurity. The PLA's more accurate short-range ballistic missiles have also resulted in more attention being paid to China in Japan's missile-defence priorities.

For India, Pakistan remains a major concern, but it too has started to look upon China's growing naval range as a long-term challenge to its maritime supremacy in the Indian Ocean. New Delhi has shown its uncertainty by dispatching troops and various advanced military systems to its eastern security frontier. Australia's strategising has moved away from its preoccupation with the Indonesian archipelago to the impact of China's military overhaul on the stability of the Pacific.

The most visible signal of Canberra's concern was the decision of the administration of then-Prime Minister Rudd to invest in various major new conventional arms systems. Russia continues to categorise the United States as the most important long-term military threat, and it has sought to strengthen cooperation with Asian allies to prepare for an anticipated confrontation between China and the US. Vietnam, finally, worries more than ever before about China's military assertiveness in the South China Sea.

For the six protagonists, insecurity has been on the rise because of a combination of factors, namely: the recognition of China's growing military strength, the proximity of China's military presence to borders or vital sea lanes, the recognition of new weapons with offensive capabilities that can be used beyond Taiwan, the uncertainty about whether China will continue to develop peacefully and last, but certainly not least, doubts about the reactions of other powers.

The balance of military power has started to tip towards China. Given its economic growth, it will continue to modernise its armed forces, but in spite of similar views of the balance of power, Japan, India, Russia, Australia and the ROK differ in their calculations of the balance of threat. Geographical proximity, the degree of offensiveness of modernising military capabilities and expected intentions are key variables that inform perceptions and policy choices about whether to engage the rising power as a threat, alone or in an alliance, or to align with it.[108] Perceptions of the rising power's intentions in turn depend on recent experiences, historical memory and the degree of congruence in terms of political identities.[109] The table above presents an overview of these conditions that influence decisions about whether to engage or whether to embrace China's military rise.

China's military rise is most negatively received in Japan and India. These two countries have the most compelling reasons for balancing China's military power. They find that Beijing is developing capabilities that can be offensively used against them; both have had recent encounters with the Chinese

Table 2. **Views of China's military power as a threat**
2 indicating applicable, 1 partially applicable and 0 not applicable.

	India	Japan	Vietnam	ROK	Russia	Australia
Recognition of military power	2	2	2	2	2	2
Proximity	2	1	2	1	1	0
Offensive modernisation	2	2	2	0	1	0
Malevolent intentions	2	2	1	1	1	1
Recent negative experiences	2	2	2	0	0	0
Negative experiences in the past	2	2	2	2	0	0
Political incongruence	2	2	0	2	0	2
	14	13	11	8	5	5
Presumed outcome	Balancing	Balancing	Balancing	Hedging	Hedging	Hedging

military: India along the disputed boundary and Japan in the East China Sea. Indeed, recent evolutions in their defence planning have demonstrated that Japan and India have taken measures that are visibly and exclusively aimed at the PRC. They have modernised their bases close to China. India has done so in the northeast and near to the Malacca Strait. Tokyo has decided to refurbish its facilities on the southern islands near to the East China Sea and Taiwan. Both countries have concentrated on China in the geographic distribution of new major weapon systems, and both have increasingly focused on confrontations with the PLA in military exercises. India is, therefore, likely to continue to fortify its border with China, to develop sufficient naval power to defend its maritime sphere of influence, and eventually to develop the capability to cut off Chinese supply lines in retaliation for aggression. Japan prioritised the defence of its southern islands and the East China Sea, and so can be expected to allocate more defence spending for the modernisation of its navy and for defence against air or missile strikes. Australia, the ROK and Russia have observed China's military modernisation, but are less worried about its future intentions or its new military capabilities. None of them has had negative encounters with the Chinese armed forces in the last decade. As a consequence these countries have displayed more reluctance in aiming their own military capabilities at China. They have all resorted to hedging. Seoul, Canberra and Moscow have launched ambitious military-modernisation programmes, but while they consider that major armed contingencies between regional powers would likely involve China, they refuse to target it directly.

CHAPTER FOUR

Towards a New Asian Security Order?

The United States remains the only military power with a truly global scope. Despite its progress in the first decade of the twenty-first century, China will probably not be able to exceed this global force-projection capacity in the next one to two decades. However, that has not prevented it from challenging America's military hegemony in Asia. It has been consolidating its asymmetric deterrence against US maritime preponderance, while incrementally developing an arsenal for distant power-projection. No other Asian power is close to accruing the financial reserves that China is channelling into its military-modernisation programmes. If the trend of official defence expenditure between 2000 and 2007 is extrapolated, by 2020 China's spending will probably equal that of Japan, India and Russia combined. The superstructure of regional security will thus become increasingly bipolar, but there will be a multipolar sub-structure in which the other powers make their independent choices about whether to balance, hedge or jump on the bandwagon. An important question, then, is whether the growing concerns in the region allow the US to build a new security alliance with India, Japan, Korea and Australia.

Such a 'hub and spokes' formation would conserve the bipolar structure. But if these powers refuse to ally with the US and independently try to keep on par with China's military power, then a shift towards a multipolar order is inevitable. Regional stability will, of course, be affected by emerging patterns of alliance.

On 4 September 2007, a flotilla of 25 vessels, including three aircraft carriers, gathered in the Andaman Sea to stage one of the largest multilateral exercises ever organised in Asia. Besides the United States, which deployed 13 warships, the *Malabar*-2007 drill was joined by the navies of Australia, India, Japan and Singapore. As this showcase of military power took place along China's most important shipping lanes, the message for Beijing seemed to be clear: if it continued to enhance its military prowess, the other countries would work together and find sufficient Chinese vulnerabilities to keep it in check. Only a few days later the Chinese government formally asked Tokyo and Delhi for an explanation.

News reports speculated about an emerging Asian NATO or a new version of the San Francisco System – which defined Japan's role in the post-Second World War order – established this time to contain China. Yet, if such an alliance was indeed emerging, the attempt to set it up soon ran into nationalistic resistance and strategic restraint.

India

Having beefed up its military ties with Washington, including a landmark ten-year defence framework agreement signed in 2005, followed by an agreement on nuclear cooperation in 2008 and a logistic support agreement in 2009, India appeared to be strengthening its bilateral relationship with the US. But New Delhi's fixation with military self-reliance and its perception of its role as a great power, together with widespread anti-

Americanism in the political elite, confidence about its favourable geopolitical position along vital sea lanes and its historically strained relations with America all continued to stand in the way of an alliance with the US. Indian defence experts and officials consider such agreements to be a matter of selective cooperation, instead of jumping on America's bandwagon. Indian officers explained that the invitation to Australia, Japan and Singapore to participate in the 2007 *Malabar* exercise was intended to firm up India's position as a naval protagonist in South Asia and not to herald a new US-led bloc against China.[1] New Delhi has since stepped up its efforts to develop what it calls multi-directional strategic relations. In 2007, it signed a defence arrangement with Canberra that foresaw more high-level defence exchanges, the exchange of information on terrorism, and maritime cooperation against piracy and other non-traditional threats.[2] With Japan, it has carried forward cooperation between coastguards. In 2008, it inked a new agreement on space security that included clauses on the defence-related use of missile, satellite and ballistic-missile defence technology. A key supplier of military technologies, Russia has remained one of Delhi's main military partners. But in spite of the increasing interaction and the conclusion of various new cooperation protocols, Indian spectators reckon Indo-Russian military relations to be a dormant strategic partnership.[3] For the long term, both sides are expected to have a joint interest in keeping China in check, but diverging views of the nature of the Chinese threat will probably continue to impede consensus and confine military synergies to the technical and commercial level. The multi-directional nature of India's security strategy has been confirmed by its increased interaction with the Chinese armed forces. In 2003 and 2007, the Chinese and Indian navies exercised together. In 2007, 2008, and 2010 joint manoeuvres were organised between the armies.

Japan

In 2010, when concerns about China's alleged assertiveness had reached new heights, Japan pressured Washington to stand strong. As indicated on page 82, Japanese Prime Minister Naoto Kan publicly recognised the importance of the American military presence in Asia at the 2010 APEC summit. Furthermore, Japan backpedalled on its request to make significant cuts in its base-hosting contributions. 'I believe that with the changing circumstances in security, the importance of host-nation support at this point is growing,' Chief Cabinet Secretary Yoshito Sengoku told the press.[4] However, this apparent policy shift does not imply that Tokyo abandoned its initial reservations about the alliance with the United States. Like earlier governments, Kan's ruling Democratic Party (DPJ) expressed disquiet about the state of the military partnership with the US. Kan was set to put into practice the main foreign-policy objectives of the DPJ, namely to establish an autonomous diplomatic strategy while developing a more equitable partnership with the US. The administration would continue to look for options to reduce the costs of America's military presence to the Japanese treasury and the Japanese citizens around the American bases.

Caught between nationalism and strategic pragmatism, Tokyo played on popular resentment at home by saying that the alliance was not balanced or that Washington was not committed enough, while at the same time trying to attract America's attention to its security concerns by highlighting regional threats.[5] The objective to build a more mature and balanced partnership implied firstly that Tokyo expected to be treated as an equal in its alliance with Washington and that the latter should take its security concerns towards China seriously, including the dispute over the Senkaku/Diaoyu Islands. Secondly, it implied that Japan would continue its drive to diversify its strategic relations, a policy that was set in motion during Shinzo Abe's short-lived premiership between 2006 and 2007. In 2007, Tokyo and Canberra agreed on an ambitious security declaration, the first with a country other than the US. It included cooperation regarding border security, counter-terrorism, disaster relief and exchange of strategic assessments.[6] In October 2008, Japan took an important step in enhancing its military cooperation with India, when the two countries signed a security declaration that involved more joint defence exercises, policing the Indian Ocean and military-to-military exchanges on terrorism. In October 2010, the Indian and Japanese premiers agreed to further expand security cooperation and to coordinate on maritime security, including freedom of navigation. In an interview with Yonhap news agency in November 2010, Kan said that Japan and South Korea had 'reached a stage to think about cooperation in the security sector'.[7] Japan would build up its own military capabilities to counter China and deploy a larger share of its troops in the south.

This raises an important dilemma for Japan: although beefing up its armed forces would be a logical response to China's military rise and could compensate for its declining economic and political status, a country with an stagnant economy might not have the financial resources to do so under its own steam. Ultimately Tokyo has the option of developing a nuclear deterrence capacity as a 'cheap' solution. Its stocks of plutonium permit the production of hundreds of warheads and in 2003, 2005 and 2006 it successfully tested a three-stage solid fuel missile. But, as the only state to have been the target of nuclear attack, Japan would have significant political and psychological hurdles to overcome before it could face joining the nuclear club. Since it is unlikely to pursue its own nuclear deterrent, Japan's quest for status and security under pressing financial limitations means itwill continue to value the security alliance with the US. At the same time, these circumstances are behind its moves to independently develop strategic relations with other regional powers and to allocate a larger part of its limited defence budget to deal with specific threats coming from China.

Australia

Australia has been one of the United States' closest military allies since the signing of the ANZUS defence pact in 1951. Both countries have continued to deepen cooperation, leading to an important agreement in 2005. This document included the establishment of a joint combined training centre, regular calls of American B-52, B-1 and B-2 bombers to Australia, more intensive joint military training and the construction of expeditionary bases at Bradshaw in northern Australia and Yampi Sound in the northwest. It has also been reported that the Bradshaw facility will accommodate C-17 aircraft and 750 supporting military personnel. At the same time, however, the notion of a China threat has been subjected to critical scrutiny.[8] China's military modernisation did not start the Australian debate about the importance of the alliance with America. But it certainly accelerated it and added an important new dimension, namely how much and how visibly Australia should engage in US-led strategies to counterbalance China.[9] The most striking expression of this came at a press conference in Beijing in 2004, when Foreign Minister Alexander Downer cast doubts over Australia's treaty obligations. He pointed out that it should not be taken for granted that Australia would side with the US in the event of a cross-strait conflict: 'The ANZUS obligations could be invoked only in the event of a direct attack on the United States or Australia. So some other activity elsewhere in the world ... does not invoke it.' In spite of Prime Minister John Howard's rush to reassure Washington that Australia would keep all options open – calculated ambiguity, as Canberra called it – this statement was followed by several other events that exposed Australia's growing reservations. While the Howard administration was in full support of participating in the American missile-defence programme, it insisted that this project should not target China. Another important evolution was the growing emphasis on self-reliance in Australia's military planning. During the short-lived tenure of Prime Minister Kevin Rudd, the 2009 Defence Paper stated: 'In terms of military power, our defence policy means that we must have the capacity to act independently where we have unique strategic interests at stake, and in relation to which we would not wish to be reliant on the combat forces of any foreign power.'[10]

South Korea

The Republic of Korea has also begun to consider other aspects of its security, outside the alliance with the US. This has not gone unnoticed in China. 'As for the ROK–US military partnership, it is a leftover from history,' a Chinese official stated at a press briefing. 'We should not view, treat or handle today's international and regional security issues with an outdated mentality.'[11] Many Koreans would endorse this view. While South Korea has been fearful of being left alone with its enemy in the north, it has been as much apprehensive of becoming a hub in possible American containment strategies against China. A poll in 2008 found that that 34% of Korean army cadets called the US the main enemy of South Korea.[12] In the past, the US maintained around 35,000 troops to watch the Democratic People's Republic of Korea (DPRK), but especially since the previous presidency of Roh Moo-hyun (2003–2008), Seoul has become more vociferous in determining the terms of the military alliance. This led to a paradoxical situation. On the one hand, the South Koreans felt that the US had a historical responsibility to maintain its presence. When Washington announced in 2004 that it would withdraw 12,500 soldiers, the ROK cried foul and accused it of unilateralism and creating a security vacuum. A similar reaction followed the decision to deploy additional units in Afghanistan and Iraq. On the other hand, Seoul has sought to impose stricter rules and a more symmetrical alliance.

The main source of disagreement has been the approach to the North. The current and previous South Korean governments favoured 'sunshine' and a peace and prosperity policy that emphasised engagement with North Korea, while the George W. Bush administration favoured a more hardline approach to Pyongyang. Apart from that, both sides were at odds over whether the American troops' mission should also include operations beyond Korea or Northeast Asia.[13] Seoul approved renewed plans to integrate American and Korean military structures, but opposed Washington's intention to use facilities in Korea to deal with a wider range of traditional and non-traditional security threats. President Roh asserted his country's right to prohibit US forces stationed in the ROK from participating in conflicts that it does not support. The Korean government also made an appeal for restraint vis-à-vis Taiwan and refused to join in the American missile-defence programme.[14] 'We need to talk to each other more, rather than talk about each other,' former Foreign Minister Song Min-soon said, referring to the option of counterbalancing China. The explanation for this quandary is that Seoul wants to gain more autonomy in its security policies but lacks the financial resources to do so. Stationing US troops in the ROK costs the Pentagon between $15 billion and $20bn annually, which is as much as the entire South Korean defence budget. Seoul has been paying for a growing share of America's soldiers, but this share has remained well below 30% of the total bill. The alliance with the US has thus become more and more driven by pragmatism instead of a strategic consensus on how to tackle the many security challenges in Northeast Asia. It remains to be seen whether the more aggressive North Korean approach, exemplified by the *Cheonan* incident in 2010, will alter this trend.

Hence, there has been no grand security alliance in the making focussed around the US. Even since 2000 when, Asian nations reacted to a more assertive China by appearing once again to close ranks around the US, this embrace remained very cautious and undetermined. This is because none of the countries that are close to Washington wants to be subjugated to a kind of Asian NATO. Both public and political perceptions of America's military presence are bleak, to say the least. During and particularly since the Cold War, these countries have also been developing their own strategic vision of the regional security order. Independent security strategies have become an important part of their new national awareness. Regional powers are also wary of becoming entangled in grand coalitions. Each country has its individual pragmatic motivations to continue to work with the US, but does not want to be seen as openly ganging up against China. The aim is to keep all the options open and avoid polarisation, while gaining as many concessions from the US as possible, even by subtly and tactically playing up the China threat. For its part, Washington has not been keen on turning the short-lived quadrennial security initiative of 2007 into a permanent structure. Prompted by the global economic crisis of 2008, Secretary of Defence Robert Gates and the new Barack Obama administration clearly prioritised pragmatic economic cooperation with China above building a strategic alliance against China.

At the same time, there is a fear of abandonment. It is clear that in the short term neither the regional powers nor the US wants to balance China collectively, but in the long run

America's partners are not convinced of its reliability as a balancer. This concern was strengthened especially during the first year of the Obama administration. These attitudes were somewhat corrected in 2010, when the US signalled its willingness to further engage China on the issues of freedom of navigation and military transparency, as a response to China's apparent military assertiveness. But even with China building up its military power and showing less restraint in using it, and incentives for collective balancing thus being increased, cooperation will probably continue to be complicated by a lack of trust in the US and differences in reactions between the cautious and the bold. The consequence of this reluctance to participate in a new grand security alliance means that the security outlook in Asia will increasingly be determined by the interplays between regional powers. The US can try to influence these dynamics, but it cannot control them. What then are the repercussions for regional stability?

Any successful Chinese deterrence strategy towards the US requires the build-up of Beijing's conventional military power in the Pacific and the extension of power-projection capacity beyond the first island chain. While Washington will not have to fear being overwhelmed any time soon, Japan understandably does have this concern. China's growing clout in the western Pacific will threaten Japan's commercial lifelines, its EEZ and ultimately its economic centres onshore. What Beijing perceives as conventional counter-force deterrence towards America is viewed by the Japanese as a counter-value threat. The main collateral effect of China's aim to counterbalance the US in East Asia is that it forces Japan into an awkward secondary position. Military polarisation will make it more difficult for Japan to hedge its bets and to avoid choosing one camp over the other unless it harnesses its own deterrence. Certainly if Japan continues to distrust

America's resolve, or if these escalating threat perceptions fuse with nationalism, insecurity will reach such a pitch that Tokyo will try to build its capabilities to maintain a sufficient degree of strategic autonomy. It will probably further expand its naval force and demonstrate its determination in or near to the disputed areas of the East China Sea. But building an enhanced naval programme will be hard for a country with a stagnating economy. This limitation might lower the threshold for going overtly nuclear. In both the conventional and nuclear scenario, military competition and patriotism increasingly threaten to spiral out of control.

It remains to be seen how India, Russia and Australia will respond. These three powers are less affected by Beijing's forays into the Pacific, but what will matter for them is how China uses military power to back its growing economic interests in Asia. China has started to explore the options for responding to non-traditional threats abroad.[15] Here it suffices to summarise that Chinese economic projects in Asia and Africa have faced an increasing number of threats emanating from local instability. Among scholars, officials and politicians, a consensus is developing that Beijing has to be more vigilant in safeguarding its stakes abroad. In December 2004, President Hu Jintao gave a seminal speech in which he stated that the Chinese military should protect the country's growing interests overseas. The actual means to secure overseas interests were assessed to be inadequate. In December 2006, a plenary meeting of the Central Committee pored over the issue of China's foreign interests and concluded that to protect these 'it should integrate various means: political, economic, intelligence, military'.[16] In 2008, President Hu asserted that the army should improve the capability to deal with a multitude of traditional and non-traditional threats and among others 'prepare itself for non-war military operations'.[17] It was striking to see how quickly Chinese experts abandoned their traditional restraint in discussing the need for military means to back up China's 'go-global' strategy. In an interview with Japan's *Asahi* newspaper, scholar Wang Jisi from Peking university presented a clear summary of China's concerns:

> Sometimes we have to use military force to solve a local problem, for instance, to rescue Chinese citizens from being kidnapped and to protect some communication line if the line is threatened by piracy or some terrorist groups. We are depending more and more on oil and natural gas supplies and other natural resources imports from all over the world, from Sudan to Angola to Venezuela to Chile. So there are communication lines China is concerned about. There are sea lanes not only through the Malacca Straits, but also through the Persian Gulf, the Indian Ocean, the Pacific Ocean and Central Asia. Military forces are needed.[18]

The first indications were emerging of a more proactive use of military means to protect economic interests. Most notable of course was the decision to dispatch a flotilla to the Gulf of Aden, but China has also signalled that it will beef up its military cooperation with key economic partners who face internal security problems. This has been the case with Pakistan and Myanmar in South Asia, and in recent years, domestic pressure to engage in Central Asia has also increased. Referring to the safety of Chinese companies in Afghanistan, Zhang Xiaodong, an expert from the China Academy of Social Sciences (CASS) explained that China 'would not continue to sit on its hands' if the security situation in Central Asia deteriorates.[19] 'China is still not doing enough,' a commentator wrote in April 2009 in the *Nangfang Daily*. 'It is not a good thing that Russia and

America dominate Afghanistan.'[20] In 2008, PLA Chief of Staff Chen Bingde reportedly stated that China 'can send troops to Central Asian countries to combat terrorist and separatist forces' if local governments ask it to do so.[21] In November 2009, a senior officer announced that China could start looking for overseas bases to support its navy mission in the Gulf of Aden, although the Ministry of Foreign Affairs later withdrew this.[22]

China's traditional distrust of the other powers' intentions impedes multilateral coordination in tackling non-traditional threats. At a June 2010 conference in Oslo, Zheng Hong of the PLA Naval Research Institute asserted that: 'On the one hand non-traditional security threats are the best hope for countries to enhance trust and to overcome the military security dilemma, but the lack of mutual trust will also limit the development of cooperation on non-traditional security threats.'[23] In the case of Myanmar and Pakistan, China has barely coordinated its policies with India. There have been a few official dialogues about drug trade, the political transition in Myanmar and the problem of terrorism in Pakistan, but these exchanges did not produce collaboration.[24] Similar problems have occurred with Australia. In Timor Leste, China has become a key economic player, but it has neglected to communicate with neighbouring Australia about political and security concerns. During widespread fighting in Dili in May 2006, Beijing and Canberra had hardly any interaction on how to deal with the escalating situation. China evacuated its citizens. In the years after, China has stepped up its attempts to gain access to the island's natural resources and also expanded its military cooperation. It built a new defence headquarters and supplied military equipment, including two patrol boats. This support neglected Australia's request for restraint in backing the new Timorese armed forces. At the height of Canberra's tensions with the government of Papua New Guinea, China weighed in with new business deals and a new defence cooperation agreement in late 2005. Beijing also ignored the sanctions imposed by Australia and the US on the military junta that seized power in Fiji in 2006. It not only sent several investment delegations to the island states, but also provided more than $160m in financial aid and established closer military relations.[25]

In Central Asia, the Shanghai Cooperation Organisation (SCO) has long been considered a platform for security cooperation with Russia, but Moscow still inclines towards defending its security interests bilaterally. It promoted the Central Security Treaty Organisation (CSTO) as an alternative to the SCO and has made headway with expanding its military presence. In 2009, an agreement was signed with the Kyrgyz government for the opening of a second base near to the strategic Fergana Valley. Russia reportedly also approached Tajikistan to open a second base on its territory, near the Afghan border, and started talks with Turkmenistan for a naval base on the shores of the Caspian Sea. None of this happened in coordination with the SCO or China directly. Chinese state media expressed concern about this evolution, with the state-controlled *People's Daily* even stating that Moscow should abandon its 'mentality of empire' and 'work with other parties'.[26] Likewise, most Chinese analysts confirmed the need for Sino-Russian security cooperation in Central Asia, and accused the Kremlin of going solo.[27] Authors like Yang Yun have stressed the destabilising impact of US involvement in the region, arguing that in spite of security interdependence the reality is more like a 'zero-sum game' with Russia trying to defend its traditional sphere of influence.[28] CASS scholar Xing Guancheng warned that a base race in Central Asia between America, India and Russia would 'create a potential security threat in neighbouring countries'.[29] Hitherto, China has refrained from establishing its own bases, but it has shored up bilateral security cooperation and there is growing domestic pressure to do more – with the SCO if possible, without it if necessary.[30]

The failure of regional organisations to tackle security challenges and the intermingling of non-traditional with traditional rivalries will probably make China less reluctant to protect its interests abroad. This assertiveness, combined with persistent instability in Asia, increases the risk of contagion from economic competition to military contest. Local elites will continue to play the regional powers off against each other to secure their position and, therefore, demand military support in return for economic concessions. As the regional powers, India and China in particular, experience more pressure to secure access to other Asian markets, they become more inclined to accede to these demands.

The development of their military industries will be an additional motivation to explore military partnerships and to export arms. In an atmosphere of distrust, arms trade heighten the stakes in a zero-sum game. Often it cannot be distinguished whether arms sales are due to commercial interests, the wish to quell unrest or the desire to counterbalance other powers. Military aid allows elites to suppress domestic security problems instead of solving them. This in turn exacerbates grievances, strengthens resistance and ultimately increases the risk of state failure. In such a scenario, the foreign allies of the beleaguered regimes will probably become the target of violence. In countries such as Afghanistan, Myanmar and Pakistan, Chinese and Indian citizens have come under fire from insurgents who accuse them of supporting discrimination.[31] Severe escalation of such violence could lead local governments to ask for more military support. In cases of complete destabilisation, it is most probable that the regional powers will use force to secure their interests. Regardless of whether this happens under a UN mandate, the lack of trust and coordination between the protagonists creates a risk that such interventions could turn failed states in Asia into frontlines of great-power contest.

Nationalism is another complicating factor. Trade ambitions might exacerbate the risk of military contest in third countries, but if the regional powers fail to realise their economic objectives, this would most likely lead to a shift from constructive nationalism to negative nationalism, in which military prestige takes a central position. Constructive nationalism identifies status with socioeconomic progress to be achieved through positive-sum international cooperation and integration.[32] Negative nationalism sees the pursuit of status as a zero-sum game, and aims at national unity by highlighting the need to compete with other states. If the nascent trading nations fail to reap the benefits from globalisation needed to maintain domestic stability, or to shore up the political centre's legitimacy, they may be tempted to gain prestige by mobilising their societies against external challengers. Attention would then move away from development to other sources of status, such as military strength. Militarism can be revived at any moment.[33] Calibrated deterrence strategies, as they develop between the regional powers, could transform into unpredictable tit-for-tat games and aggressive signalling. It is not axiomatic that the economies of China and India will continue to boom. Japan is stuck in an inflationary trap and is struggling to revive economic growth, while Russia too has suffered a long period of slow growth.

The gradual erosion of America's military preponderance in Asia will increase the risk of a regional great-power contest. Insecurity among the Asian protagonists may become more compelling and its consequences more unpredictable. Even if a security dilemma between two players is mitigated because they attain an acceptable military equilibrium, the balance with a third state might be disturbed, with the latter's countermoves disturbing the equilibrium between the first two. Frictions will be aggravated, because growing economic presence abroad invariably instigates powers to extend their military range, certainly if the US became less able to keep this evolution in check. In this case there will a greater risk of rivalry in third countries or in maritime spaces like the Indian Ocean. Security dilemmas, as well as arms races, will thus reinforce each other, particularly in a context where negative nationalism looms large.

Possible flashpoints and conclusions

Asia's new security order will be multi-layered, which makes it difficult to forecast specific conflicts. Instead, it is more useful to analyse how a more powerful China might seek to address existing sources of insecurity and what this would imply for other protagonists. The aim of doing so is not to predict whether certain conflicts will occur, but to evaluate what kind of responses could be triggered by security threats in Asia's changing strategic landscape.

As a consequence of the altering military balance, China might be less reluctant to use force against Taiwan if the recent rapprochement does not lead to a settlement of the island's political status that is acceptable to Beijing. Thus far, since the Third Taiwan Strait crisis in 1995 and 1996, which followed a series of missile tests conducted by the PRC in the waters around the island, four main elements have kept the peace. Firstly, there was sufficient restraint in Taipei not to cross the red line of secession. Secondly, China believed that it could win over Taiwan if it waited long enough and provided incentives for mainland-friendly interest groups. Thirdly, China realised that its stance on Taiwan would be an important pillar of the good-neighbour policy (*mulin zhengce*). Finally, China was not confident that its military capabilities were strong enough to effectively punish Taiwan and to deflect possible counter-measures. If the rapprochement with the incumbent Kuomintang administration fails and Beijing considers that this unique window of opportunity for peaceful reunification is closed, it would undoubtedly opt for a tougher line, thereby increasing the risk of escalation. Building up and upgrading its military capabilities will make China much more confident that it has the military upper hand in the Taiwan Strait and that it can control escalation in the event of US intervention.

If deterrence fails and the US were to show its flag in the vicinity of Taiwan, China could first opt for sea-denial operations by laying mines in Taiwanese ports to block supplies, by positioning conventional submarines in the shallow waters around the island and by dispatching surface combatants in the Taiwan Strait. The second step would probably be to use electronic warfare to disturb communications and to reduce the reliability of important weapons systems like missiles. Should America sail into the Taiwan Strait or try to give military aid to Taiwan, China could retaliate indirectly with precision strikes on Taiwanese targets or by provoking limited incidents that force the US into the role of aggressor and lower the threshold for China to potentially use force against US targets. In the future, such brinkmanship will be more effective, not only because China possesses the platforms and command structures to deploy its armed forces in a calibrated way in a high-tech environment, but also because it can ultimately rely on local military superiority should tit-for-tat posturing escalate into war. After 15 years of constructive engagement towards Taiwan, the Chinese government will also be more under pressure to save face when the rapprochement runs aground or reverses. It will be prepared to go much further than it did in 1996 to test America's resolve by staging denial operations and even the option of an all-out war becomes more probable.

The fact that the US Navy enjoys such superiority in the blue waters of East Asia will not discourage China from trying to close the gap. There is a growing willingness to venture deeper into the Pacific and China is developing the necessary means for this. The more it shows its flag in the blue waters of East Asia, the more the United States will want to demonstrate that it is not deterred by staging large exercises or by patrolling more intensively in the green waters around China. This will not only bring about a new arms race, but also increase the risk of incidents, particularly because of the lack of proper communication between the two countries' armed forces and because of China's relative inexperience in long-range patrolling with submarines or aircraft. But the high seas of the Pacific are not Taiwan, which obviously remains a much higher strategic priority. Thus, political elites on both sides will not want to risk escalation in the Pacific. But in this case too, their final decisions might be shaped as much by nationalism and turf wars between political and military elites, as by pragmatic calculations of strategic interests. The most immediate consequence of a military build-up in the Pacific will be that it sustains hostile perceptions, which could spill over into other regions or forms of warfare. Power plays in the Pacific will almost certainly complicate international efforts to address flashpoints elsewhere in South and Central Asia, Africa and the Middle East. China and America might also want to compensate for the vulnerability of their conventional forces by developing deterrence in space, enhancing electronic-warfare capabilities or preparing cyber strikes.

China's military modernisation could also determine how intra-state conflicts in Asia will be addressed. While political stability in most Southeast Asian countries improved, the risk of instability has grown in Afghanistan, the DPRK, Laos, Myanmar, Nepal, Pakistan and most Central Asian countries.[1] In most of these states economic inequality, corruption, ethno-religious tensions and the scarcity of natural resources are likely to further aggravate domestic tensions or even to cause state failure.[2] China is thus surrounded by a corridor of uncertainty. Many of these countries will continue to be important political partners and host a growing number of Chinese investors in the sectors of natural resources, construction, trade, etc. Thus far, China has avoided becoming embroiled in its neighbours' complex domestic problems. At best it has diversified its local political contacts, but in essence it has continued to back political elites to maintain stability with economic aid and military support. In spite of suspicion of the intentions of other powers, Beijing preferred to let them bear the costs of fighting terrorism and repressing unrest in the restive area around Afghanistan. China confined its direct involvement to keeping its expatriates informed of potential calamities, enhanced intelligence-gathering and occasional programmes for military training. But as economic interests in these countries expanded, China began to define domestic problems in other Asian countries in security terms, thereby possibly legitimating a more robust response to these threats, including military action. This could simply be a matter of preparing evacuation plans for Chinese citizens in hostile conditions. The PLA has already begun intensive simulations based on this scenario.

The change of attitude towards stabilisation missions could lead China to send troops to protect important facilities or trade corridors. As such this does not have to lead to rivalry with other powers. The governments of unstable states might actually invite it to help maintain stability. But communication about troubled Asian states with countries like the United States,

India, Japan and Russia remains poorly developed. It is also doubtful that regional organisations will be coherent enough to coordinate responses, should serious violence break out. It is unclear whether a consensus could be reached within the United Nations Security Council or whether possible mandates to intervene will be clear enough to avoid tensions between the intervening countries. Distrust can be further aggravated when powers have diverging objectives and support opposing parties within a conflict zone. In this way, troubled states could evolve into frontline states, in which the intervening powers struggle for control, using peacekeeping as a pretext for their presence there.

Another possibility is the escalation of border disputes, not least in China's maritime periphery. Even as the naval balance alters in China's favour, it will not necessarily use power offensively to enforce its claims. But it could be less reluctant to exploit the riches of disputed waters. This has already been the case with the Chunxiao gas field, fishing around the Spratly Islands and even tourism on the Paracel islets. This would lead to more distrust of China's ultimate intentions and perhaps even prompt other countries to stage more frequent patrols, thereby increasing the risk of skirmishes. A better armed China, conscious of the need to stand strong on its territorial integrity, will undoubtedly be less reluctant to retaliate.

On land, the border with India remains a possible flashpoint. As long as no agreement is reached on the demarcation, the two countries will have to show their resolve in large swathes of no-man's land. Despite the agreement to demilitarise the Line of Actual Control, both sides have patrolled more frequently in disputed areas. Because the two countries are able to inflict severe damage on each other, the threshold to use force in the border area is high and this will probably remain so. To avoid incidents, Beijing and New Delhi also vowed to enhance their communication. For the short term, mutual deterrence significantly reduces the chance of a border war and freezes the territorial predicament. But in the long run, military build-up will continue to fuel distrust, provoke further military modernisation and motivate the two sides to develop alternative sources of deterrence. For China, this would mean strengthening the alliance with Pakistan, while India may aspire to possess a denial capacity in the Indian Ocean. With a potential resurgence in nationalism, or competition for scarce water resources especially in the Himalayas, eroding the stabilising effect of deterrence, the border conflict faces an uncertain future.

Conflicts over natural resources and borders tend to be mutually enforcing. China has experienced serious water shortages, leading to drought in rural areas and supply problems in large cities. As a consequence, it intensively exploited rivers and other natural water reserves, some of which it shares with neighbouring countries further downstream. China has frequently been accused of stealing water from Bangladesh, India, Kazakhstan, Laos, Myanmar and Vietnam. As many of the Himalayan glaciers will melt rapidly as a consequence of global warming, rivers will transport less water to riparian areas in the future, making Chinese dams and irrigation projects upstream a very probable target for criticism. Excluding India, none of the countries that share water resources with China will have the leverage to compel it to respect water-sharing agreements, nor could they threaten to use force to ensure that agreements are honoured. For India too, the costs of starting an armed conflict over access to the water reserves of the Himalayas will be higher than the possible benefits. But if no sharing settlement can be reached diplomatically, the domestic political costs of backing down would certainly increase drastically for any administration, because a conflict over water will almost certainly coincide with heightened tensions in Jammu and Kashmir, and Arunachal Pradesh. A conflict over water would almost certainly force India on to the defensive to avoid losing natural resources that are key to its domestic development. This could lead New Delhi to step up its military presence in Arunachal or in Jammu and Kashmir, to which China could respond by sending more troops to the frontier, fortifying sensitive facilities along rivers in the border zone, and even by deploying its new high-altitude helicopters and aircraft. A lot will depend on the political climate in both countries, but such posturing could spiral out of control.

Discussing the territorial disputes, Shi Xiaoqin, a scholar at the Academy of Military Science, said: 'Emotion and [reason] are part of the same balance. You cannot decouple them.' Whereas the focus on domestic economic development has mitigated tensions over the border in the past two decades, economic needs tend to exacerbate rivalry over water resources in the border area. Territorial and economic conflicts also tend to be inextricably linked in the fishery sector. As a consequence of the insatiable demand for sea food, the Chinese fishery fleet has become the largest in Asia, operating all over the Asian seas. They often compete with fleets from other countries. On several occasions, navies from Indonesia, Vietnam, South Korea and the Philippines have used force to expel Chinese poachers, triggering protests in China and outrage among the Chinese blogging community. Acts of fishery patriotism like these often ignite territorial tensions, as many of the incidents occur in disputed waters. In the future, a combined deployment of unarmed patrol ships and navy vessels will have to deter such actions and eventually intervene.

These are the main sources of insecurity on which China's growing military power could have an impact. In all of them, other countries in the region will perceive China's defensive force posturing as offensive. The altering balance of power will almost certainly lower the threshold of using force to protect its interests vis-à-vis Taiwan, in maritime economic and territorial conflicts with smaller countries and to counter instability in failing states that threaten its key regional interests. In these scenarios, China will think that it has a better chance of winning a military conflict and that the costs no longer outweigh its economic benefits. This more assertive use of military power will also be prompted by the growing demands on natural resources, the awareness of China's status and the persistent domestic pressure to act determined. China's growing confidence in its military power will also make it more resolved to defend its interests against India, Japan and the United States. But as the costs of using force here remain extremely high, Beijing will prefer to avoid collision and diffuse its deterrence across other areas or less lethal aspects of warfare. But if this diffusion fails and its challengers continue to mobilise on highly sensitive conflicts, China would likely show its resolve, driven by nationalism and the confidence that it can strike back.

China will not outstrip US military preponderance in Asia any time soon, but it has started to modernise its armed forces in a way that will significantly reduce America's manoeuvrability in the Pacific. Certainly, it has been struggling to translate its newly gained technological capabilities into tangible operational capacity, but it is learning fast and there is no reason to assume that China will not overcome the many obstacles on the path from a mass army to an advanced combat force. The main objective for Beijing remains to influence the course of events, should an armed contingency within its littoral periphery occur. Thus far it has managed to substantially raise the cost for the United States to intervene in Chinese coastal waters, essentially by deploying denial capabilities onshore and near shore. It is now preparing to move from coastal defence to offshore deterrence, and from purely asymmetric deterrence towards the development of conventional means for naval power projection. Growing financial limitations are creating ever-increasing difficulties for the US in responding to China's rise. The key to assessing China's progress is not to see whether it drives the US out of the Pacific, but the extent to which it is able to fill the gap between defencelessness and launching an all-out war. In other words, what matters most is escalation control and military brinkmanship, both of which will be needed to flexibly deter the US from using military force to determine the outcome of conflicts in China's mainly maritime environment.

This will not only depend on the direct relations between the two protagonists, but also on how the emerging bipolar superstructure affects the multipolar substructure. While China is essentially building up its military power to engage the United States, the other regional powers look at China for their security strategies. None of them commands the same financial power as Beijing in modernising its armed forces, but most of them are developing specific military niches. While China's growing military power can be expected to prompt external balancing with the US, the prevailing posture has been to hedge. Cooperation with America has increased, but so has interaction with China. A grand alliance with Washington at its centre is unlikely, because of the fear of entanglement, a lack of confidence in Washington's reliability as an ally and the ambition to attain regional leadership. The three main dangers of unchecked military competition between the Asian powers are that growing interests abroad could bring about an extended range of military power projection, that the interests to protect economic stakes abroad can spark military contest in third countries, and that such tensions could easily become the subject of negative nationalism if economic growth fails to produce the expected gains in national unity and stability.

Washington must tackle four related problems. Firstly, it will have to choose between counterbalancing China and trying to persuade it to use its military power in a cooperative way. To do this, it must address Chinese suspicions that America is reaching out with one hand, while supporting Chinese enemies with the other. In 2009 the PLA Chief of Staff offered an example of this contradictory stance: 'The United States has sought China's help in international operations such as the war in Afghanistan or in fighting piracy off Somalia, but undermined the mutual trust needed for such cooperation with its arms sales to Taiwan,' he said. 'Once the United State needs us to cooperate, they are good to us, they are friendly to us. Otherwise, they can do anything they want, even to offend the Chinese people. But I don't think that kind of cooperation can continue.'[3]

The US also has to recognise that it is not the only power to which Beijing adapts its policies. Even if it tries to change Chinese strategy, its attempts are destined to fail if other regional powers pull Beijing into a military contest. If Washington opts to counter China's military rise, and this brings us to the third problem, it will increasingly experience the tension between showing resolve and effective deterrence. Showing resolve would mean that it sticks to harnessing Taiwan and maintaining its presence near to China's shores. But given the PLA's growing dominance in this area, this traditional focus of deterrence might not be the most cost-effective. A cheaper form of deterrence would be to concentrate power where China is the most vulnerable, notably along its economic lifelines in South Asia. The final problem arises as a consequence to another potential US strategy. Should it begin to find the costs of deterring China too high, Washington can opt for a divide-and-rule strategy towards the regional powers. If one or more protagonists challenge China, this could force Beijing to reorient its deterrence and eventually even exhaust it. The danger, however, is that such regional rivalry could become uncontrollable and spill over into other areas.

For Beijing, the main challenge will be to prevent the quest for security from causing more insecurity or endangering its development. For financial and strategic reasons, China has restrained its military modernisation during the first decades of its economic take-off, but in the second decade of the twenty-first century, it will almost certainly shift its military build-up into a higher gear. It is natural that a rising power with growing interests will also grow in terms of military clout; but for a new protagonist, the pursuit of military modernisation could appear more overtly hostile. China's military strategising has essentially been an extension of defensive realist thinking, but defensive moves have a great risk of being perceived by other states as offensive provocations.

As if this were not enough to be dealing with, Beijing needs to understand the importance of how it handles the transition from a weak army, and a policy of concealment towards a strong army, and growing confidence in showing its capabilities. The deployment of new submarines in the wake of American aircraft carrier, the unannounced launch of an anti-satellite missile, the dispatching of warships in the Indian Ocean without reassuring New Delhi, and the construction of an aircraft carrier are just a few examples of how overly bold muscle flexing can strengthen speculation about offensive intentions. To effectively defend its growing interests, Beijing must balance the benefits of attaining status and prestige in its military capabilities with the potential threat to its long-term security should it convey hostile intent or provoke an arms race.

The current Asian scramble for multidirectional confidence building and ad hoc military exchanges hardly mitigates distrust. The best we can hope for in the middle-to-long term is the development of a concert of Asian powers, including the United States. Similar to the Quintuple Alliance in nineteenth-century Europe, such a concert would involve frequent informal meetings to identify major security challenges and coordinate solutions.

It could be developed gradually, starting with meetings between low-ranking officials focusing on specific challenges. One of the most significant features of concert-like coordination is inclusive balancing. External or exclusive balancing strategies isolate, strengthen antagonistic perceptions among states and often exacerbate hostile attitudes on the part of the power that is targeted. Inclusive balancing, on the contrary, does not aim at targeting a particular power, but at sanctioning particular behaviour. Concerts are open to all major powers as long as they coordinate their security policies, contribute to stability and show restraint. Military adventurism is sanctioned collectively and could lead to expulsion by the other members. Inclusive balancing offers the advantage that common non-traditional security threats help mitigate traditional threats among states in a structured way. It reflects multipolarity and gives equal status to all regional protagonists, but its informal decision-making process allows the evolving distribution of power to be taken into account. It helps develop personal relations and trust between officials and political leaders. For Washington, inclusive balancing could help avoid the high costs of traditional containment or confrontation, while reassuring its traditional allies. For China, coordination with the other powers would be vital in reducing the burden of securing its growing interests abroad, tempering the suspicion of its rise and raising the costs for the others – particularly India and Japan – to resort to an aggressive unilateral military build-up.

However, for the long run a concert is no guarantee of peace if dramatic changes in the Asian balance of power occur. The most important trend to watch here is the development of the Chinese economy and the extent to this translates into military capacity. If its military modernisation continues to accelerate, it will not matter so much for the others what China actually does, but what it *could do* with its growing prowess. And even if the PRC were to limit the commissioning of new military systems, it would suffice that other countries believe it has the knowhow to produce advanced arms. Expected power is at least as important as actual power.

In the coming decades, if the gap in military power continues to close, there could be a moment when the US calculates that it has to stop China's eastward expansion in the Pacific before it becomes unstoppable. For the Asian powers, China's economic growth will lead to a choice between joining it and opposing it more fiercely. If one country decides to move closer to China, others may either follow or feel more pressured to keep a distance and resort to internal balancing. In the end, it will not be the quality of interaction that determines stability in Asia, but the change in the distribution of material capabilities and the aptitude to convert them into influence. When changes in the balance of power become so fundamental that states are forced to completely revise their policies, it will not matter how the challenger behaves at that point in time, but rather how it *could* behave in the future. Worst-case scenarios will then ultimately be the likeliest bet.

GLOSSARY

AWACS	Airborne Warning and Control aircraft
APEC	Asia-Pacific Economic Cooperation
ASEAN	Association of Southeast Asian Nations
CAS	China Academy of Science
CCS	Command and control system
CEP	Circular Error Probable (indicator of weapon's delivery accuracy)
CICIR	China Institute for Contemporary International Relations
CIISS	China Institute for International Strategic Studies
CPR	Centre for Policy Research (India)
CSTO	Central Security Treaty Organization
C4I2	Command, control, communication, information and intelligence
DPRK	Democratic People's Republic of Korea
DRDO	Defence Research and Development Organisation (India)
EEZ	Exclusive Economic Zone
FOS	Forward operating site
ISDA	Institute for Defence Studies and Analyses, India
IRBM	Intermediate-range ballistic missile
JFN	Joint Fires Network
JMSDF	Japan Maritime Self-Defense Force

JTAGS	Joint Tactical Ground Station
KORCOM	US-Korea Command
LDP	Liberal Democratic Party (Japan)
MIRV	Multiple independently targetable re-entry vehicles
PACOM	US Pacific Command
PLA	People's Liberation Army
PLAAF	People's Liberation Army Air Force
PLAN	People's Liberation Army Navy
PLANAF	People's Liberation Army Navy Air Force
PRC	People's Republic of China
PSI	Proliferation Security Initiative
ROK	Republic of Korea
SOSUS	Sound Surveillance System
SCO	Shanghai Co-operation Organization
UAV	Unmanned aerial vehicles

NOTES

Introduction

1   Conversation with Department of Defense official, Washington, 13 December 2008.

2   Tony Capaccio, 'China's New Weapons May Threaten US Bases, Ships, Gates Says', *Bloomberg*, 19 September 2009.

3   See, for example, Kevin Cooney and Sato Yoichiro (eds), *The Rise of China and International Security* (London: Taylor and Francis, 2008); Michael Swaine, Andrew Yang and Evan Medeiros, *Assessing the Threat: The Chinese Military and Taiwan's Security* (Washington DC: Carnegie Endowment for International Peace, 2007); Dennis Blasko, *The Chinese Army Today: Tradition and Transformation for the 21st Century* (London and New York: Routledge, 2006).

4   Ministry of Foreign Affairs, *China's Position Paper on the New Security Concept*, Ministry of Foreign Affairs, 31 July 2002.

5   See Wang Yizhou, 'Quaqiu Zhengzhi He Zhongguo Waijiao' (Beijing: Shijie Zhishi Chubanshe, 2003), pp. 247–50; Zhang Yunling, 'Interdependence in World Economy', *Ouzhou Yanjiu*, April 1998, pp. 1–10; Zhang, 'Zonghe Anquan Guan Ji Dui Wo Guo Anquan De Sikao', *Dangdai Ya Tai*, January 2003, pp. 1–16; Pang Zhongying, 'Ling yi Zhong Quanqiu Hua', *Shijie Jingji yu Zhengzhi*, February 2001, pp. 5–10.

6   Yang Yi, 'Peaceful Development and Strategic Opportunity', *Contemporary International Relations*, vol. 16, no. 9, 2006.

7   Xia Yafeng, 'The Study of Cold War International History in China: A Review of the Last Twenty Years', *Journal of Cold War Studies*, vol. 10, no. 1, 2008, pp. 81–115.

8   *Ibid.*

9   Robert Zoellick, 'Whither China: From Membership to Responsibility', speech at the National Committee on the United States and China Relations, presented in New York, 21 September, 2005, available at http://www.vub. ac.be/biccs/site/assets/files/Education/ Zoellick.pdf.

10 Statement of Admiral Timothy Keating before the Senate Armed Services Committee on US Pacific Command Posture, 24 March 2009, http://www. pacom.mil/web/pacom_resources/

pdf/19MAR09 PACOM SASC Posture Statement.pdf.

[11] Robert Jervis, *Perception and Misperception in International Politics* (Princeton, NJ: Princeton University Press, 1976), in particular chapter 4; Stephen Walt, 'Alliance Formation and the Balance of World Power', *International Security*, vol. 9, no. 4, 1985, pp. 4–41.

[12] Mark Sparrough, Interview with David Shambaugh, 2003, available at: www.cdi.org.

[13] Sun Shangwu , 'PLA Not Involved in Arms Race', *China Daily*, 2 February 2007.

[14] State Council, *China's National Defense in 2008*, Information Office of the State Council of the People's Republic of China, Beijing, January 2009, chapter 1.

[15] David Shambaugh, *Modernizing China's Military* (Berkley, CA: University of California Press, 2002) pp. 4 and 289; also *China's National Defense*, 2006, 2007, and 2008, chapter 1.

[16] Wang Jisi, 'Meiguo Baquan Yu Zhongguo Jueqi', *Waijiao Pinglun,* October 2005, pp. 13–16.

[17] See, for example, Ni Shixiong and Wang Yiwei, 'Baquan Junshi: Lengzhanhou Meiguo De Zhanlue Xuanze', Fudan University, 6 November 2006; Men Honghua, 'Guoji Jizhi Yu Meiguo Baquan', in Hu Angang (ed.), *Jiedu Meiguo Dazhanlue* (Hangzhou: Zhejiang People's Publishing House, 2003), pp. 138–57; Zhu Shida, 'The Rise of China and the Sino-US Relations', *International Outlook*, Spring 2006.

[18] Wang Zaibang, 'Strategic Balance in the Asia-Pacific Region', *Contemporary International Relations*, vol. 17, no. 4, 2007.

[19] For theoretical interpretations, see Ken Booth and Nicholas Wheeler, *The Security Dilemma: Fear, Cooperation and Trust in World Politics* (London: Palgrave, 2007); Jervis, 'Cooperation under the Security Dilemma', *World Politics*, vol. 30, no. 2, 1987, pp. 167–214; John Herz, *Political Realism and Political Idealism* (Chicago, IL: Chicago University Press, 1987).

[20] Jervis, *Perception and Misperception in International Politics*, pp. 96–111; Glenn Snyder, *Deterrence and Defence: Toward a Theory of National Security* (Princeton, NJ: Princeton University Press, 1976), p. 4; Alexander George and Richard Smoke, *Deterrence in American Foreign Policy: Theory and Practice* (New York: Columbia University Press, 1974), pp. 16–18.

Chapter One

[1] Avery Goldstein, *Rising to the Challenge: China's Grand Strategy and International Security* (Stanford, CA: Stanford University Press, 2005), p. 203.

[2] These are part of the Chengdu and Lanzhou Military Region, which count a combined total of 400,000 troops.

[3] Taylor Fravel, *Strong Borders Secure Nations* (Princeton, NJ: Princeton University Press, 2008).

[4] Shambaugh, *Modernizing China's Military*, p. 66.

[5] Mark Ryan, David Finkelstein and Michael McDevitt, *Chinese Warfighting:*

The PLA Experience Since 1949 (Armonk, NY: M.E. Sharpe, 2003), p. 125.

6 Jack Snyder, *The Soviet Strategic Culture: Implications for Limited Nuclear Operations* (Santa Monica, CA: RAND, 1977), p. v.

7 Alastair Ian Johnston, *Cultural Realism: Strategic Culture and Grand Strategy in Chinese History* (Princeton, NJ: Princeton University Press, 1998), p. 250.

8 Andrew Scobell, *China's Use of Military Force* (Cambridge and New York: Cambridge University Press, 2003), p. 193.

9 Michael Pillsbury, *China Debates the Future Security Environment* (Washington DC: National Defense University Press, 2000). See also Bonnie Glaser, 'China's Security Perceptions', *Asian Survey*, vol. 33, no. 3, 1993, pp. 252–71.

10 Wang Jisi, 'Pragmatic Nationalism: China Seeks a New Role in World Affairs', *Oxford International Review*, Winter 1994, p. 29; see also Xu Qi, '21Shijichu Haishang Yu Zhongguo Haijun De Fazhan', *Zhongguo Junshi Kexue*, vol. 17, no. 4, 2004, p. 78.

11 Statement by Tang Jiaxuan at the General Debate of the 57th Session of UN General Assembly, 19 April 2004.

Chapter Two

1 Quoted in David Burton, *Theodore Roosevelt, American Politician* (London: Fairleigh Dickinson University Press, 1997), p. 58.

2 Alfred Thayer Mahan and Francis Sempa, *The Problem of Asia* (New York: Transaction Books, 2003), p. 133.

3 John Lewis Gaddis, *Strategies of Containment* (Oxford: Oxford University Press, 2005), p. 59; Dean Acheson, *Present at the Creation: My Years at the State Department* (New York: W.W. Norton, 1969), p. 357.

4 *Ibid.*, p. 91.

5 Gaddis, *Strategies of Containment*, p. 117; also quoted in Allen Suess Whiting, *China Crosses the Yalu* (Stanford, CA: Stanford University Press, 1960), p. 39.

6 Gaddis, *Strategies of Containment*, p. 142.

7 *Ibid.*; Michael Yahuda, *The International Politics of the Asia-Pacific* (London and New York: Routledge, 2004).

8 Nicholas Spykman, *America's Strategy and World Politics* (New Brunswick, NJ: Transaction, 2008), pp. 129–55; Zbigniew Brzezinski, *The Grand Chessboard* (New York: Basic Books, 1995), p. 151.

9 Department of Defense, *Quadrennial Defense Review*, Washington DC, 2006, pp. 14 and 30.

10 PACOM, *PACOM Strategy* (Camp Smith, November 2008), pp. 4 and 8.

11 The combined complement of VLS breaks down as follows: 12 *Ticonderoga* with 122 VLS and 28 *Arleigh Burke* with 90 VLS. See Norman Polmar, *The Naval Institute Guide to the Ships and Aircraft of the US Fleet* (Washington DC: United States Naval Institute, 2005).

12 Norman Friedman, *The Naval Institute Guide to World Naval Weapon Systems* (Annapolis, MD: Naval Institute Press, 2006), p. 107.

13 Department of Defense, 'Base Structure Report' (Washington DC: Department of Defence, 2002), Table 309A. *Idem* for 2009 version. These are conservative estimates. In 2002, 780 troops were reported to be based in Guam, rising to 4,095 in 2008. Troop levels dropped by about 26,000 in South Korea, 19,000 in Japan and 3,000 in Hawaii.

14 *Ibid*. These are conservative estimates. In 2008 troop levels were as follows: 51,264 in Hawaii, 32,459 in Japan, 27,968 in the ROK, 4,095 in Guam.

15 David Nagle, 'Blue Ridge, Hickam AFB Demonstrate Joint Fires Network Capabilities', http://www.navy.mil/search/display.asp?story_id=5569.

16 'Theater Defense: New Army Command to Stand Up in the Pacific', *Army Communicator*, Fall 2005.

17 'Construction Begins at Pearl Harbor Shipyard', *Navy Times*, 23 February 2009; 'Pearl Harbor Will Be Sub Hub', *Navy Times*, 9 January 2009.

18 Eric Talmadge, 'Guam, Focus of New US Strategy, Faces Hurdles', *Marine Corps Times*, 13 January 2009; Nichole Scott and Mark Zimmerhanzel, 'The Changing Face of an Island', *AFCE Magazine*, vol. 16, no. 1, 2008.

19 Donna Miles, 'Gates Views Massive Growth Under Way in Guam', *American Forces Press Service*, 31 May 2008.

20 Richard Burgess, 'Guam's Return to Prominence', *Sea Power*, 25 January 2007.

21 Evan Carter, 'Red Horse Squadron Moves to Andersen', *The Pacific Edge*, 2 June 2006, http://www.pacaf.af.mil/news/story.asp?id=123016945; Karen Jowers, 'Military Buildup Threatens to Overwhelm Guam', *Air Force Times*, 10 May 2008.

22 Shirley Kan and Larry Niksch, *Guam: US Defence Deployments* (Washington DC, Congressional Research Service Report RS22570, 2008), p. 3; 'Raptor Squadron Arrives at Guam', *Stars and Stripes*, 21 January 2009.

23 Commission on Review of Overseas Military Facility Structure, *Review of Overseas Military Facility Structure of the United States* (Arlington, VA: Commission on Review of Overseas Military Facility Structure), 9 May 2005, p. 283. See also Statement of Admiral Timothy Keating before the House Appropriations Committee, Subcommittee on Military Construction, 12 March 2008.

24 Toshi Yoshihara, 'Japan, Basing and America's Military Presence in Northeast Asia', paper presented at the APSA 2008 Annual Meeting, Boston, MA, 28 August 2008.

25 Allison Day, 'Joint Tactical Ground Station Opens at Misawa', 23 January 2008, www.pacaf.af.mil/news/story.asp?id=123083463.

26 Samantha Quigley, 'Commander Stresses Senate Support to Achieve Goals in Korea', *American Forces Press Service*, 8 March 2006; Fred Baker, 'Camp Humphreys Development Rises from Rice Paddies', *American Forces Press Service*, 21 June 2007.

27 Kwak Tae-hwan and Joo Seung-ho, *The United States and the Korean Peninsula in the 21st Century* (Aldershot: Ashgate, 2006).

28 Nam Chang-hee, *The Realignment of the USFK in the Military Transformation and South Korea's Defense Reform 2020* (Tokyo: NIDS, 2005), p. 7–8.

29 Emma Chanlett-Avery, *Thailand: Background and US Relations*, CRS Report for Congress, Washington DC, 2 October 2006, p. 9.

30 Congressional Budget Office, *Moving US Forces: Options for Strategic Mobility*

(Washington DC: Congressional Budget Office, 1997), chapter 4.

31 Harold Kennedy, 'Air Force Forging Alliances in Pacific Region', *National Defence Magazine*, March 2004.

32 Jung Sung-ki, 'Pullout of Apache Helicopters Causes Security Jitters', *Korea Times*, 26 November 2008; Jim Garamone, 'President Orders 12,000 Soldiers, Marines to Afghanistan', *American Forces Press Service*, 17 February 2009.

33 'US Asks Japan to Pay as Much of US$7.6 billion as Possible for Marines' Guam Move: Report', AP, 16 February 2007.

34 Kiroku Hanai, 'Costly Transfer to Guam', *Japan Times*, 23 March 2009.

35 Office of the Chief of Naval Operations, *Report to Congress on Annual Long-Range Plan for Construction of Naval Vessels for FY2009*, Washington DC, Department of Defense, February 2008, p. 16.

36 Ronald O'Rourke, 'Navy Force Structure and Shipbuilding Plans: Background and Issues for Congress' (Washington DC: CRS, 2 October 2008); Julian Barnes, 'Navy Cancels New Destroyers', *Los Angeles Times*, 31 August 2008.

37 O'Rourke, *Navy Littoral Combat Ship Program* (Washington DC, Congressional Research Service, 5 June 2009).

38 August Cole and Yochi Dreazen, 'Pentagon Pushes Weapon Cuts: New Focus on Unconventional Conflicts; Defense Contractors Gird for Political Battle', *Wall Street Journal*, 7 April 2009.

39 See, for example, Feng Liang and Duan Zhi-Ting, 'Zhongguo Haiyang Diyuan Anquan Tezheng Yu Xinshiji Haishang Anquan Zhanlue', *Zhongguo Junshi Kexue*, 2007, pp. 22–30.

40 'China Air, Naval Boost Risks Raising Tension', Reuters, 30 September 2009.

41 Cui Xiaohuo and Zhang Haizhou, 'Top Military Officers Lash Out at US Espionage', *China Daily*, 11 March 2009.

42 White Paper on National Defence, 2006, chapter 2.

43 'China Urges US to Stop Surveillance Operations', *China Daily*, 29 August 2009.

44 State Council , *China's National Defense in 2008* (Beijing: Information Office of the State Council of the People's Republic of China, January 2009), chapter 1; Xin Lei, 'Meiguo Junjian Jiejin Zhongguo Haianxian Zhanfu Daodan Weixie Dongan Yanhai', 17 October 2004, www.defence.org.cn/article-1-47226.html.

45 Quoted in Yong Deng, *China's Struggle for Status* (Cambridge: Cambridge University Press, 2008), p. 41.

46 Ye Zhicheng, 'Zhongguo Maixiang Shijie Daguo Zhilu', www.irchina.org/xueren/china/view.asp?id=251.

47 Liu Zhongmin , 'Shilun Dengxiaoping De Haiyang Zhengzhi Zhailue Sixiang', *Zhongguo Haiyang Daxue Xuebao*, April 2007.

48 See David Finkelstein, 'China's National Military Strategy: An Overview of the Military Strategic Guidelines', *Asia Policy*, June 2007, pp. 87–140.

49 Xia Chan, 'Jiang Zemin Addresses Party', *China Daily*, 17 June 1997.

50 White Paper on National Defence, 2006, chapter 2.

51 Xu Qi, '21Shijichu Haishang Yu Zhongguo Haijun De Fazhan', *Zhongguo Junshi Kexue*, vol. 17, no. 4, 2004, p. 78.

52 Wang Xiaobin, 'Haiyang Zhanlue Yu Guojia Anquan', *Ben Qi Zhong Guo Qing Nian*, April 2009.

53 Peng Guangqian and Yao Youzhi (eds), *The Science of Military Strategy* (Beijing:

Military Science Publishing House, 2005), p. 213.

54 Xu, '21Shijichu Haishang'; Feng and Duan, 'Zhongguo Haiyang'.

55 *Ibid*. For a broader discussion, see Zhang Wenmu, 'Lun Zhongguo Haiquan', *Shijie Jingji Yu Zhengzhi*, October 2003, pp. 8–14; and You Ji, *The Evolution of China's Maritime Doctrines* (Singapore: Institute of Defence and Strategic Studies, May 2002).

56 Zhanyi Xue, chapter 11, in Wang Houqing and Zhang Xingye (eds), *The Science of Military Campaigns* (Beijing: National Defense University Press, 2000).

57 See, for example, the Director of the Science and Technology Research Office of the National Defense University, interviewed by CCTV; Wu Xiaopeng, 'Zhang Shaozhong Shaojiang: Zhong-guo Haijun Zuozhan Nengli Paizai Shijie Siwuming', CCTV, 17 April 2009.

58 See Xin, 'Meiguo Junjian'.

59 For a discussion of the DWL002 Passive Radar Detection System, see *Xiandai Bingqi*, June 2009, pp. 29–31.

60 For a discussion of OTH radars, see Tao Mao et al., *Gaoping Dibo Chaoshiju Leida Tedian Ji Yingyao Yanjiu, Xiandai Leida*, March 2009.

61 Xiao Bei, 'Zhongguo Leida Budui Zai Goujian Zhoujixing', *PLA Daily*, 22 December 2008.

62 The new vessels commissioned between 2004 and 2008 are: T-094, T-093, T-039, T-051C, T-052C, T-052B, 956EM, T-054, T-054A and T-022.

63 Wu Xiaopeng, 'Zhongguo Haijun Xinxing Quzujian Peibei Xinxing Fangkong Daodan', CCTV, 15 April 2009.

64 Polmar, *Naval Institute Guide*, p. 512.

65 Lyle Goldstein and William Murray, 'Undersea Dragons: China's Maturing Submarine Force', *International Security*, vol. 28, no. 4, p. 166.

66 Park Sung-hyea and Peter Chu, 'Thermal and Haline Fronts in the Yellow/East China Sea', *Journal of Oecanography*, vol. 62, no. 5, pp. 617–38.

67 Andrew S. Erickson, Lyle J. Goldstein and William S. Murray, 'Chinese Mine Warfare: A PLA Navy "Assassin's Mace" Capability', *China Maritime Study* no. 3, June 2009, www.usnwc.edu/cnws/cmsi/publications.aspx.

68 Kenneth Allen, Jonathan Pollack and Glenn Krumel, *China's Air Force: The Long March to Modernization* (Santa Monica, CA: RAND, 1995); James Mulvenon, 'True is False, False is True, Virtual is Reality, Reality is Virtual: Technology and Simulation in the Chinese Military Training Revolution', in Roy Kamphausen et al. (eds), *The People in the PLA* (Carlisle, PA: Strategic Studies Institute, 2008), pp. 69–70.

69 Luzhou Class, *Jane's Fighting Ships* database, 8 February 2008, accessed online via the Royal Military Academy, Brussels.

70 *Ibid*. See also 'Chinese naval fire-control radars', *Jane's Naval Fire Control Radars*, 27 May 2008.

71 *Jiangkai* II (Type 054 A) class (FFGHM), *Jane's Fighting Ships* database, 5 August 2008.

72 Michael Chase, Andrew Erickson and Christopher Yeaw, 'Chinese Theater and Strategic Missile Force Modernization and its Implications for the United States?', *Journal of Strategic Studies*, vol. 32, no. 1, pp. 67–114.

73 Chen York , 'The Shifting Balance of Air Superiority at the Taiwan Strait', in Martin Edmonds and Michael Tsai (eds), *Taiwan's Security and Air Power*

(London and New York: Routledge, 2004), p. 44.

74 Zhang Wei , *Lianhe Zhanyi Zhihui Xue*, Beijing Military Science Press; Chin Lei Zhang, 'Lianhe Zhanshu Yu Hetong Zhanshu De Chayi', *PLA Daily*, 7 May 2009.

75 Andrew Erickson, 'Can China Become a Maritime Power?', in Toshi Yoshihara and James Holmes (eds), *Asia Looks Seaward* (Santa Barbara, CA: Greenwood, 2008), p. 99; Goldstein and Murray, 'China Emerges as a Maritime Power', *Jane's Intelligence Review*, 1 October 2004; Erickson, 'PLA Navy Modernization: Preparing for "Informatized" War at Sea', *Jamestown China Brief*, 29 February 2008, available at http://www.jamestown.org/programs/chinabrief/; Russell Hsiao, 'Kuayue-2009: Shifts in PLA Military Planning?', *Jamestown China Brief*, 15 May 2009. For Chinese views on key joint-force operations, see Sun Yefei, 'Zhongguo Renming Jiefangjun Jiang Zai Dongshandao Juxing Lianhe Junshi Yanxi', *Jiefangjun Daily*, 3 July 2004.

76 John Wilson Lewis and Litai Xue, *Imagined Enemies: China Prepares for Uncertain War* (Stanford, CA: Stanford University Press, 2006), pp. 77–173; Wang Zhengde, *Jiedu Wangluo Zhongxinzhan* (Beijing: National Defense Industry Press, 2004); Li Wenquan, 'Zhongguo Wangluo Zhongxinzhan Neng Lizhi Yanjiu', *Defense Journal*, vol. 23, no. 6, pp. 100–13.

77 'Qudong "Pingtai Zhongxinzhan" Xiang "Wangluo Zhongxinzhan" Zhuanxing', *PLA Daily*, 6 July 2007; 'Shujulian Zuozhan Wangluo Jiang Dianfu Chuantong Zhanzheng Linian', *Jiefangjun Daily*, 5 February 2009; Jin Sun, *Zhanshu Shujulian Jishu Yu Xitong*

(Beijing: National Defense Industry Press, 2007).

78 'Zhongguo Ziyan De Shendun Xitong Daodi You Duo Xianjin?', *Jiefangjun Daily*, 9 September 2005.

79 Richard Fisher, 'China's Naval Secrets', *Wall Street Journal*, 5 May 2008.

80 See, for example, Christopher Pehrson, *String of Pearls: Meeting the Challenge of China's Rising Power Across the Asian Littoral* (Carlisle, PA: Strategic Studies Institute, 2006), pp. 3–7.

81 Andrew Selth, 'Chinese Whispers: the Great Coco Island Mystery', *The Irrawaddy*, vol. 15, no. 1, 2007; Indrani Bagchi, 'China Eying Base in Bay of Bengal?', *India Times*, 9 August 2008.

82 Conversation with RADM RC Wijeguanarathna, Sri Lankan Navy, The Hague, 21 May 2010.

83 Conversation with retired Navy officer, Beijing, 21 September 2010.

84 *Ibid.*

85 For more on the DF-21, see Eric Hagt and Matthew Durnin, 'China's Antiship Ballistic Missile', *Naval War College Review*, vol. 62 no. 4, pp. 87–114.

86 Huang Hongfu ,' Conception of Using Conventional Ballistic Missiles to Strike Aircraft Carrier Formation', *Scientific and Technological Research*, January 2003, pp. 6–8; Huo Fei and Luo Shiwei, 'Arrows Without Bows? An Evaluation of the Effectiveness and Employment of Anti-Aircraft-Carrier Ballistic Missiles', *Modern Ships*, April 2008, p. 28.

87 Andrew Erickson and David Yang, 'On the Verge of a Game-Changer', *Proceedings*, vol. 135, no. 5, 2009.

88 The third generation of the *Red Bird* family is reported to comprise a land-based (HN-3A), a ship-launched (HN-3B) and an air-launched (HN-3C) type, all with a range of 2–3,000km. Wendy Minnick, 'China Tests New

Land-attack Cruise Missile', *Jane's Intelligence Weekly*, 21 September 2004.

89 Referred to in Gorden Fairclough, 'China Builds Up its Nuclear Arsenal', *Wall Street Journal*, 22 April 2010.

90 Robert Norris and Hans Christensen, 'Chinese Nuclear Forces', *Bulletin of the Atomic Sciences*, July 2008, p. 44.

91 Hsiao, 'China's Underground Great Wall and Nuclear Deterrence', *China Brief* vol. 9, no. 25, December 2009.

92 Zeng Pingshun, 'Xiandai Xinxi Duikang: Wangdian Yitizhan', *Jiefangjun Bao*, 7 September 2004.

93 Donna Miles, 'China Requires Close Eye as It Expands Influence, Capability', *American Forces Press Service*, 12 March 2008.

94 China does not have effective defence against long-range precision strikes originating more than 200km away.

95 I am indebted to Vijay Sakhuja for this insight.

96 Conversation with senior Chinese security expert, Brussels, 17 June 2009.

97 Liu Liang Xian, 'Meiguo Guofangbu Kaizhi Xianru "Wu Didong"', *Xiandai Junshi*, November 2008, pp. 66–71. The author claims that despite large budget constraints and the burden of two large combat operations, the DoD is continuing to make major expenditures for developing major conventional arms.

98 Jiang Yuanqing and Zou Hui, 'The Advent of a New Cold War at Sea Between China and the US', *Modern Military*, September 2008, pp. 62–6.

99 'Quanmian Fenxi: Zhongguo Haishang Zhanlue He Mei Jieru Nanhai"Daolian Zhihua"', Sina.net, 6 April 2009; Feng Liu Yu, 'Mei Weilai "Haishang Daji" Liliang Toushi', *Dangdai Haijun*, January 2009, p. 50-8.

100 Hu Xin, 'Jingzheng Yu Tiaozhan: Yazhou De Haiquan Zhizheng', *Xiandai Junshi*, December 2008, pp. 58–63, 58 and 60. 'Mei Haijun Zhiding Xinban "Haijun Zuozhan Gainian"', *Xiandai Junshi*, October 2008, pp. 15–16: The author states that the US aims at containing China from the sea front, and that Chinese cities are still prone to *Tomahawk* missiles launched from submarines.

101 Ge Wei, 'Weilai Meiguo Keneng Hui Zenyang Jieru Taihai Weiji', *Xiandai Junshi*, April 2008, pp. 57–63.

102 Xiao Yusheng, *21 Shiji Chu Daguo Junshi Lilun Fazhan Xindongxiang* (Beijing: Military Science Press, 2008); Liu Yongtao, 'Material and Identity: the Possible Future Directions of Sino-US Security and Political Relations', *SIIS International Review*, vol. 45, no. 4, 2006, pp. 46–60; Wang Jisi, 'China's Search for Stability with America', *Foreign Affairs*, September 2005, p. 40; Wang Zaibang, 'The Strategic Balance in the Asia-Pacific Region', *Contemporay International Relations*, vol. 17, no. 4, 2007.

103 Ye Zhicheng, 'Zhongguo Haiquan Bixu Congshu Yu Luquan', Xinhua, 28 March 2007.

104 Zhang Jingwei, 'Zhongguo Jueqi Zhilu Buneng Hulue Haiquan', *Guangming Ri Bao*, 28 March 2007.

105 'Zonglun 2008 Nian Haijun Wuqi Zhuangbei Fazhan Youshi: Zhuanfang Guofang Daxue Wanglei Fu Jiaoshou', *Dangdai Haijun*, February 2009, pp. 69–72; Rong Wang (ed.), *Zhongguo Diyuan Zhanluelun* (Beijing: National Defense University Press, 2006); Yan Xuetong, 'The Decade of Peace in East Asia', *East Asia*, vol. 20 no. 4, 2003, pp. 29–51; Wu Xingzuo, 'The Current State of Global Military Security',

Contemporary International Relations, vol. 17, no. 6, 2007.

106 Yang Chengkang, 'Weilai De Changgui Qian Ting', *Dangdai Haijun,* January 2009, pp. 60–7; Yu Ping, 'Wojun Xinxing Changgui Qianting Xingneng Yi Jiejin Shijie Xinjin', *Military Digest,* 6 October 2008.

107 Conversations with various defence experts, Beijing, 20–22 September 2010.

108 Conversations with CIISS fellow, Beijing, 21 September 2010.

109 'Hu Jintao Kaocha Haijun Zhu Sanya Budui Qiangdiao Tuijin Junshi Douzheng Zhunbei', *Jiefangjun Bao,* 11 April 2008.

110 Jang Feng, 'Weilai Haishang Lianhe Zuozhan Zhongtouxi Shi Shenme?', *Dang Dai Hai Jun,* November 2008, pp. 41–5; 'Zhongguo Sanjun Budui Lianhe "Zuozhan" Miji Junyan Jing Qiaoqiao', *Jiefangjun Bao,* 16 February 2009.

111 Shawn Capellano-Sarver, 'Naval Implications of China's Nuclear Power Development', in Erickson et al. (eds), *China's Future Nuclear Submarine Force* (Anapolis, MD: Naval Institute Press, 2007), p. 157. On the nuclear reactor, see p. 195. On the pump-jet system, see 'Tupo! Zhongguo Luoshenhao Chaodao Ciliuti Qianting Shiche', Xinhua, 30 July 2008. Military attachés in Beijing have also mentioned these systems in conversations about China's development.

112 Liu Zhenhua, 'Haijun Silingyuan: Zhongguo Haijun Jiang Yanzhi Xinyidai Jianting, Feiji', Xinhua, 15 April 2009.

113 Deng Jingyin, 'New Generation of Fighter Jets on Horizon', *Global Times,* 10 November 2009.

114 Joel Wuthnow, 'The Impact of Missile Threats on the Reliability of US Overseas Bases: A Framework for Analysis' (Washington DC: Strategic Studies Institute, US War College, 2005); Eric McVadon, 'The Taiwan Problem: Beijing's Arms for a Fight it Hopes to Avoid', *Armed Forces Journal,* November 2005.

115 Testimony of Admiral Gary Roughead, Chief Naval Officer, US Navy, before the House Armed Services Committee, Washington DC, 13 December 2007.

116 Testimony of Admiral Timothy Keating Commander, US Pacific Command, and General Burwell Bell, Commander, US Forces Korea, before the House Armed Services Committee On the Posture of the Pacific Command, Washington DC, 12 March 2008; see also Bruno Greg, 'Expanding US Military Partnerships in the Pacific', interview with Timothy Keating, CFR, 12 December 2008, http://www.cfr.org/publication/17994/.

117 Peter Brookes, 'The Great Wall Goes to Sea', *Armed Forces Journal,* July 2009.

118 Speech Delivered by Secretary of Defense Robert Gates, Naval War College, Newport, RI, 17 April 2009, www.defenselink.mil/speeches/speech.aspx?speechid=1346.

119 Jim Garamone, 'Gates: Sea Services Must Question Embedded Thinking', *American Forces Press Service,* 3 May 2010.

120 Jonathan Pollack, 'American Perceptions of Chinese Military Power', in Herbert Yee and Ian Storey (eds), *The China Threat: Perceptions, Myths and Reality* (London: Routledge, 2004), pp. 43–65.

121 This concerned the USNS *Victorious,* USNS *Loyal* and USNS *Impeccable.* In the case of the *Victorious* a Chinese fishing patrol boat used a high-intensity spotlight to illuminate the ship and

a Chinese Y-8 maritime surveillance aircraft circled around it. In the case of the *Impeccable,* a Chinese frigate approached the vessel without warning and crossed its bow. Two hours later, a Y-12 aircraft buzzed the ship at low altitude.

122 John Lee, 'Opaqueness at Heart of Chinese Military's U.S. Strategy', *Korea Herald,* 9 June 2010.

123 Robert Ross, 'The Geography of the Peace: East Asia in the Twenty-first Century', *International Security,* vol. 23, no. 4, 1999, p. 105.

124 Fravel, 'China's Search for Military Power', *Washington Quarterly,* vol. 31, no. 2, 2008, p. 125.

125 For an excellent historical overview, see Keith Neilson and Elisabeth Errington (eds), *Navies and Global Defense* (Westport, CT, and London: Praeger, 1995).

126 Spykman, *America's Strategy and World Politics,* p. 469.

Chapter Three

1 Jervis, *Perception and Misperception in International Politics,* pp. 180–90; Peter Katzenstein, *The Culture of National Security* (New York: Columbia University Press, 1996), pp. 15–30.

2 Denny Roy, 'Stirring Samurai, Dissaproving Dragon', in Yoichiro Sato and Satu Limaye (eds), *Japan in a Dynamic Asia* (New York: Lexington, 2006), pp. 69–89; Taoka Toshitsugu, *Tujie Riben Wei Junshi Li Guotu* (Tokyo: Naka Tsune Publishing, 2003); Masashi Nishihara, 'Major Changes Since mid-2006 in Summary', *RIPS Policy Perspectives,* May 2007; Hideaki Kaneda, Kazumasa Kobayashi, Hiroshi Tajima and Hirofumi Tosaki, *Japan's Missile Defense: Diplomatic and Security Policies in a Changing Strategic Environment* (Tokyo: The Japan Institute of International Affairs, 2007), p. 117; Joshua Rowan, 'The US–Japan Security Alliance, ASEAN, and the South China Sea Dispute', *Asian Survey,* vol. 45, no. 2, 2005, pp. 414–36.

3 Kenneth Pyle, *Beyond Japan* (New York: Public Affairs, 2007), pp. 321–3.

4 Japanese Ministry of Defense, *The Defense of Japan* (Tokyo: Ministry of Defence, 2008) p. 3. A detailed assessment of the PLA follows on pp. 43–58. See also Ogawa Shinichi (ed.), *East Asian Strategic Review* (Tokyo: The National Institute for Defence Studies, 2008).

5 Japanese Ministry of Defense, *The Defense of Japan* (Tokyo: Ministry of Defence, 2009), p. 33.

6 Sakurai Yoshiko, 'Security of Japan and Japanese Expressing Concerns', *JFSS Quarterly Report,* October 2008.

7 Jodie Allen, *A New Leader for a Chronically Gloomy Japan,* Pew Global Attitudes Project, 22 September 2008, http://pewresearch.org/pubs/960/a-new-leader-for-a-chronically-gloomy-japan.

8 The Chicago Council on Global Affairs, *Asia Soft Power Survey* (Chicago, IL: Chicago Council on Global Affairs, April 2009), p. 15.

9 Ozawa's statement was made during a closed lecture given in the southern City of Fukuoka in April 2002. It was not intended to be made public.

10 Pyle, *Beyond Japan*, p. 215; Mike Mochizuki, 'Japan's Shifting Strategy Toward the Rise of China', *Journal of Strategic Studies*, vol. 30, nos 4–5, 2007, pp. 739–79.

11 Alto Taku, *Japan's Asia diplomacy: Ideas for the 21st century*, Policy Paper no. 323 (Tokyo: IIPS, March 2007).

12 The Defence of Japan, 2008, Part 3, pp. 22–3

13 'China, Japan to Hold Joint Naval Drill', Xinhua, 28 November 2009.

14 The Defence of Japan, 2008., Part 2, p. 108.

15 *Ibid.*, Part 2, p. 203–214

16 'Japan Gets Helicopter Carrier', *Straits Times*, 19 March 2009.

17 'Helicopter Carrier Commissioned: MSDF's Largest Combat Vessel May Raise Concerns within Asia', *Japan Times*, 19 March 2009.

18 Kosuke Takahashi, 'Japan Frets over the US's F-22s', *Asia Times*, 5 February 2009; Wendell Minninck, 'Japan AF Expands Definition of "Defense"', *Defence News*, 14 July 2008.

19 'Defense Plan Prepared for Remote Islands', *Japan Times*, 16 January 2006.

20 Christopher Hughes, 'Japanese Military Modernisation: In Search of a Normal Security Role', in Ashley Tellis and Michael Wills (eds), *Strategic Asia 2005–06: Military Modernisation in an Era of Uncertainty* (Seattle, WA: National Bureau of Asian Research, 2005), p. 121; White Paper 2008, p. 141.

21 *Ibid.*, p. 140.

22 'Japan May Deploy Troops Near Disputed Islands', *Japan Times*, 2 July 2009.

23 'Ministry of Defense to Station 100 GSDF Members on Island in Okinawa to Observe China', *Mainichi Daily Times*, 10 November 2010.

24 Thomas Christensen, 'China, the US–Japan Alliance, and the security Dilemma in East Asia', *International Security*, vol. 23, no. 4, 1999, pp. 49–80.

25 Joint Statement of the US–Japan Security Consultative Committee, Washington DC, 19 February 2005, www.mofa.go.jp/region/n-america/us/security/scc/joint0502.html.

26 Toshio Yamagishi and Hokkaido University, 'Uncertainty, Trust, and Commitment Formation in the United States and Japan', *American Social Journal*, vol. 104, no. 1, 1998, pp. 165–94

27 Koji Murata, 'Do the Guidelines Make the Japan–US Alliance More Effective?', in Masashi Nishihira (ed.), *The Japan–US Alliance: New Challenges for the 21st Century*, (Tokyo: Japan Center for International Exchange, 2007), pp. 19–38; Shimakawa Masashi, *The Security Alliance with the US, and America's Military Strategy in East Asia* (Tokyo: Social Critics, 2006); Sunohara Takeshi, *A Changing Alliance* (Tokyo: Nikkei, 2007).

28 Takashi Hoshiyama, *The Improving Course of Japan-China Relations and the Role of the US*, Policy Paper no. 329 (Tokyo: IIPS, September 2008).

29 Kotani Tetsuo, 'China's Aircraft Carrier programme', *RIPS' Eye*, 6 March 2009; 'US Marines Relocate to Guam, Japan Asked for 500 Million Yen', *Yomiuri Shimbun*, 28 June 2008.

30 Kaneda et. al., *Japan's Missile Defense: Diplomatic and Security Policies in a Changing Strategic Environment*, p. 135.

31 Sueo Sudo, 'Toward a Japan–US–ASEAN Nexus', in Masashi Nishihara (ed.), *The Japan-US Alliance*, p. 109; 'Flagging Japan–US Alliance: Bilateral "Marriage" Needs Injection of Vigor', *Daily Yomiuri*, 27 January 2009; 'Growing Criticism on the Obama

Admininstration's Focus on China', *Nikkei*, 28 April 2009.

32 Yuka Hayashi, 'Kan Backs U.S. Military Role in Asia', *Wall Street Journal*, 13 November 2010.

33 Jonathan Holslag, 'The Persistent Security Dilemma between India and China', *Journal of Strategic Studies*, vol. 32, no. 6, 2009, pp. 811–40.

34 'China Building Maritime Battlefield Around India', *Daily Excelsior*, 2 December 2006.

35 'China Now Bigger Threat than Pak: IAF Chief', *Hindustan Times*, 23 May 2009.

36 T.D. Joseph, 'Military Modernisation in China: Some Implications for India', *Air Power*, vol. 3, no. 1, 2006, pp. 89.

37 Jagannath Panda, 'India and China on Parade', *Asia Times*, 1 August 2007.

38 Quoted in David Blair, 'India Must Not Show Weakness to China', *The Telegraph*, 13 September 2008.

39 Brahma Chellaney, 'Increasing Challenges to Stability in Asia', *The Hindu*, 10 January 2009.

40 'Natha Lu Amidst Guns and Roses', *Himalaya Review*, 11 June 2007.

41 'Sukhoi Base in the East to Counter China', *Times of India*, 28 September 2007.

42 Bappa Majumdar, 'China in Mind, India to Boost Eastern Air Power', *Straits Times*, 8 August 2007.

43 Nitin Gokhale, 'India Ups Vigil on China Border', NDTV, 26 May 2009.

44 Santosh Patnaik, 'Navy to Have Second Base Near Vizag', *The Hindu*, 17 September 2009; 'Navy Gearing up to Meet Coastal Security Challenges', *The Hindu*, 29 March 2009; 'Eastern Fleet to be Expanded', *The Hindu*, 24 March 2009; Integrated Headquarters Ministry of Defence, *India's Maritime Strategy*, Directorate of Strategy, Concepts and Transformation, Integrated Headquarters Ministry of Defence (Navy), New Delhi, May 2007.

45 Archana Masih, 'IAF Air Base Rises from Tsunami Wreckage', *Rediff*, 24 June 2005.

46 Bobo Lo, *Axis of Convenience: Moscow, Beijing, and the New Geopolitics* (London and Washington DC: Chatham House and Brookings Institution Press, 2009), pp. 74–9; Alexander Lukin, 'Russian Perceptions of the China Threat', in Herbert Yee and Ian Storey (eds), *The China Threat* (London: Routledge, 2002), pp. 86–115; Vladimir Skosyrev, 'Kitai gotovitsia k Bolshoi Voine', *Nezavisimaya Gazet*, 21 January 2009; Y. Vedernikov, 'Krasnyi Drakon: Covremennye Voennomorski Sili', (Vladivostok: Morkniga, 2007); *Itogi s Vladimirom Putinym: Krizis i Razlozhenie Rossiiskoi Armii* (Moscow: Institute of National Strategy, November 2007), pp. 12–14.

47 A. Skvortsov and D.A. Kruglikov, 'Tendentsii Izmeneniia Soderzhaniia Voennykh ugroz Voennoi Bezopasnosti Rossiiskoi Federatsii na Srednesrochnuiu Perspektivu', in S.N. Grinyaev (ed.), *Voennaia Bezopasnost' Rossiiskoi Federatsii v XXI veke* (Moscow: General Staff of the Armed Forces, Center for Military and Strategic Studies, 2004), p. 132.

48 M.L. Titarenko, *Rossiia, Kitai i Drugie Strany Azii*, (Moscow: Forum Publishers, 2008).

49 Sergey Luzianin, *Rossiia i Kitai v Evrazii* (Moscow: Forum Publishers, 2009).

50 E. Kabulov, 'Kitaiskaia Ugroza Tsentral'noi Azii', *Info Asia*, 25 June 2008.

51 Ajdar Kurtov, 'Neodnoznachnost Aktivnosti Kitaia v Tsentral'noi Azii',

Political News Agency of Kazakhstan, 7 December 2006.

52 Herman Dudchenko, 'Kitai i Dal'nii Vostok Rossii: K Voprosu o Demograficheskom Disbalanse', *Vestnik Evrazii*, March 2002, pp. 142–9.

53 On the evolution of the overall perceptions, see Alexander Lukin, *Russia's Image of China and Russian–Chinese Relations* (Washington DC: Brookings Institution Press, 2004).

54 Russian National Security Council, *Strategiia Natsional'noi Bezopasnosti Rossiiskoi Federatsii do 2020 Goda*, National Security Council, Moscow, 12 May 2009, paragraphs 18–20.

55 *Ibid.*, paragraphs 11, 41 and 42.

56 Yuri Kitten, 'Udar po Rossii Skoro Mozhet Stat Realnostiu', YTPO.ru, 18 May 2006.

57 Andrei Kokoshin interview: 'Voennaia Doktrina Rossii Dolzhna byt' Izmenena', 14 March 2007, www.point.ru/news/stories/5208. See also Andrei Kokoshin, 'O Sisteme Strategicheskogo Upravleniia v KNR' (Moscow: Institute of International Security Problems, Russian Academy of Sciences, 2001).

58 Yevgeny Bazhanov, 'Kitai: Partner, Ne Ugroza', *Moscow Times*, 29 March 2009. See also S.A. Karaganov, 'Sovremennyi Kitai: Vyzov ili Vozmozhnosti?', *Rossiia v Globalnoi Politike*, March 2004.

59 'General Gareev: Rossiia Meniaet svoiu Voennuiu Doktrinu', Ria Novosti, 16 January 2007; M.A. Gareev, 'Strategicheskoe Cderzhivanie: Hovaia Kontseptsiia Boennoi Bezopasnosti Rossii', *Red Star*, 8 October 2008.

60 Andrei Piontkovsky, 'Kitai Gotovitsia k Bolshoi Voine', *Project Syndicate*, 3 September 2007.

61 For a lengthy interview with Konstantin Sivkov, see the *Russian Reporter Magazine*, 26 August 2008, www.rusrep. ru/interviews/2008/08/21/154050.

62 Alexander Hramchihin, 'Kak Kitai Razdavit Rossiiu', Political news Agency, 23 July 2008; Hramchihin, 'Pochemu Kitai Slomaet ves' Mir', Political News Agency, 10 July 2008; Hramchihi, 'Kitai: Budushchaia Voennaia Sverkhderzhava', *Nezavisimaya Gazeta*, 27 March 2009.

63 Artur Blinov, 'Geopoliticheskie Stsenarii Paraga Khanny', *Nezavisimaya Gazeta*, 29 April 2009.

64 Alexey Muraviev, *The Russian Pacific Fleet* (Canberra: Australian Maritime Affairs Seapower Centre, 2007); 'Kuda idet Rossiiskii Flot?', *Kommerssant*, 25 February 2008.

65 Igor Korotchenko, 'Baza Atomnykh Podvodnykh Lodok v Viliuchinske Zgdet Strategicheskie Raketonostsy "Borei"', *Pravda*, 28 August 2008; 'Mironov Schitaet Razvitie Morskikh Strategicheskikh sil Osobo Vazhnoi Zadachei', *Kommerssant*, 5 August 2008; 'Mooring Float for Russian Navy Set Off from Khabarovsk to Kamchatka', *Vladivostok Times*, 7 August 2007.

66 'Novyi Avianosets Planiruetsia Vvesti v Sostav TOF v Blizhaishie Desiat Let' Ria Novosti, 27 October 2008.

67 'Polety na Su-24M2 Nachali Piloty polka v Pereiaslavke Khabarovskogo Kraia', 25 January 2008, www.army.lv/ ru/su-27/100/11344.

68 'V Krasnoznamennom Dal'nevostoch-Nom Obedinenii VVS i PVO Uspeshno Proverili Sistemu PVO', Ria Novosti, 19 September 2008.

69 Leonid Nikolaev, 'Park Sovremennykh Istrebitelei VVS Rossii Segodnia i k 2015 Godu', *The Republic*, May 2009.

70 Australian Department of Defence, 'Defending Australia in the Asia Pacific Century: Force 2030',

Department of Defence, Canberra, June 2009, p. 49.

71 Interview with Australian defence official, Brussels, 2 September 2009.

72 Fergus Hansen, *The Lowy Institute Poll* (Canberra: The Lowy Institute, 2008), p. 12.

73 'Unique Naval Exercise Underway', *Australian Defence News*, 24 September 2010.

74 Department of Defence, *Australia's National Security: A Defence Update to 2020* (Department of Defence, Canberra, 2005), pp. 5–6.

75 *Ibid.*, pp. 19-21.

76 *Ibid.*, . 63.

77 *Ibid.*, p. 37.

78 James Holmes and Toshi Yoshihara, 'Mao Zedong, Meet Alfred Thayer Mahan: Strategic Theory and Chinese Sea Power', *Australian Defence Force Journal*, no. 171, 2007, p. 43; Robert Ayson, 'Asia's China Strategy: A Perspective from Australia', Paper Presented at the 3rd Berlin Conference on Asian Security, SWP, 17–19 September 2008, p. 4.

79 Paul Dibb, *The Future Balance of Power in East Asia: What are the Geopolitical Risks?* SDC Working Paper no. 406, January 2008, p. 5. See also William Tow and Russell Trood, *Power Shift: Challenges for Australia in Northeast Asia* (Barton: Australian Strategic Policy Institute, 2004).

80 Hugh White, 'The Limits of Optimism; Australia and the Rise of China', *Australian Journal of International Affairs*, vol. 59, no. 4, 2008, p. 478.

81 Strahan Lachlan, *Australia's China: Changing perceptions from the 1930s to the 1990s* (Cambridge: Cambridge University Press, 1996), p. 289; Ron Huisken (ed.), *Rising China: Power and Reassurance* (Canberra: ANU Press, 2009); Roy Campbell, *Howard's Long March: The Strategic Depiction of China in Howard Government Policy, 1996–2006* (Canberra: ANU Press, 2009).

82 Department of Defence, *Force 2030* (Canberra: Department of Defence, 2009), p. 52.

83 'Australia to Boost Defence to Keep Pace with Asian Buildup', *Financial Express*, 2 May 2009.

84 Interview with Australian official, Brussels, 2 September 2009.

85 Conversation with senior Australian diplomat, Brussels, 13 September 2009.

86 David Kang, *China Rising* (New York: Columbia University Press, 2008), p. 105; Kang, 'Between Balancing and Bandwagoning: South Korea's Response to China', *Journal of East Asian Studies*, vol. 9, no. 1, 2009, pp. 1–28; Kang, 'South Korea's Embrace of Interdependence in Pursuit of Security', in Ashley Tellis and Michael Wills (eds), *Strategic Asia 2006–2007: Trade, Interdependence, and Security* (Washington DC, NBR, 2006), pp. 139–170. See also Kim Taheo, 'South Korea and a Rising China: Perceptions, Policies, and Prospects', in Yee and Storey, eds., *The China Threat*.

87 Chicago Council of Global Affairs, *Global Views 2006* (Chicago, IL: Chicago Council of Global Affairs, 2006), p. 36.

88 Yashuhiru Matsuda, 'Japanese Assessments of China's Military Development', *Asian Perspective*, vol. 31, no. 3, 2007, pp. 183–93.

89 The Chicago Council on Global Affairs, *Asia Soft Power Survey* (Chicago, IL: Chicago Council on Global Affairs, April 2009), pp. 14 and 15.

90 Kim Byung-kook, 'Caught in between Rising China and Hegemonic America: South Korea's Search for a Grand Strategy', presentation at the Department of Political Science, Korea

University, January 2006; See also Lee Chung Min, 'China's Rise, Asia's Dilemma', *The National Interest*, 22 September 2005.

91 On President Lee's attitudes towards China, see Han Sukhee, 'From Engagement to Hedging: South Korea's New China Policy', *Korean Journal of Defence Analysis*, vol. 20, no. 4, 2008, pp. 335–51; Scott Snyder, 'China-Korea relations in the Lee Myung-bak Era: Mixed Picture for China Relations', *Comparative Connections*, April 2008; and Jae Ho Chung, 'Jungug Gunsa Ryeogui Jonghap Jeog Pyeongga' (Seoul: Korean Institute for Defence Analyses, 28 August 2006). This assessment asumes that China will catch up with America's military supremacy by 2030. Lee Tai Hwan, a prominent scholar from the Sejong Institute, acknowledges the PLA's many shortcomings but stresses that China has altered the maritime balance of power in the East and South China Seas. See Lee Tai Hwan, 'Junggug Gunsa Ryeogui Jeunggang ui Bunseok gwa Jeonmang', *Policy Study*, no. 1, 2007, pp. 154–74; Kim Tae Ho, Director, Center for Contemporary China Studies at Hallym University, has presented an overview of the impact of China's naval, air force and missile capacities. See Kim Tae-ho, '21 Shiji Zhonguo Haiyan Zhanlue Weilai Zhan Gouxiang', paper published online by Hallym University, April 2008; Kim, Gang Nyeong Kim, 'Changes in our Military Environment and Korea's Security', *The Army*, no. 248, 2002, pp. 24–35.

92 2006 White Paper, Korean Ministry of Defence, Seoul, p. 12.

93 Lee Sang-hee, 'Korea's Role in Global Security', speech delivered at the Shangri-La Security Dialogue, Singapore, 30 May 2009, www.mnd.go.kr/mndEng/AboutMND/profile/speech/20081002/1_3600.jsp.

94 Rob Taylor, 'China Arms Spend Prompts South Korea Arms Race Warning', *The Star*, 5 March 2009.

95 Sunny Lee, 'How to Mend Ties between S. Korea and China?', *Korea Times*, 1 November 2010.

96 'Most S. Koreans Skeptical About Cheonan Findings, Survey Shows', *Chosun Ilbo*, 8 September 2010.

97 Conversation with South Korean official, Brussels, 14 September 2010. See also Kim Heungkyu, *Post-Cheonan Regional Security* (Seoul: Institute of Foreign Affairs and National Security, 2010).

98 Luo Yuan, 'Big Brother Flexes Muscles', *China Daily*, 31 July 2010.

99 Edward Wong, 'China's Disputes in Asia Buttress Influence of US', *New York Times*, 22 September 2010.

100 Lee, 'Junggug Gunsa Ryeogui Jeung-gang ui Bunseok gwa Jeonmang', p. 165.

101 These options were tabled at a conference organised by KIDA in May 2007. See Park Ihn-hwi, 'Sino-Japan Strategic Rivalry and the Security of the Korean Peninsula', *Korean Journal of Defence Analysis*, vol. 19 no. 1, 2007, pp. 79–102; Bruce Bernett, *A brief Analysis of the ROK's Defence Reform Plan*, (Santa Monica, CA: RAND, 2006), pp. 10 and 13; 'Edward Olson, US-DPRK Relations', Kwak Tae-Hwan (ed.), *The United States and the Korean peninsula in the 21st Century* (Aldershot: Ashgate, 2006), p. 154.

102 *Ibid.*; also implied by the 2006 Defence White Paper, pp. 8 and p. 12.

103 Sheen Seong-Hoo 'Out of America, Into the Dragon's Arms?', in Kevin Cooney and Yoichiro Sato (eds), *The*

Rise of China and International Security (London: Taylor and Francis, 2008), p. 148; Bernett, *A brief Analysis of the ROK's Defence Reform Plan*, p. 8.

104 Yul Yoo Chan, 'North Korea's Resurgence and China's Rise: Implications for the Future of Northeast Asian Security', *East Asia*, vol. 25, no. 3, 2008, pp. 293–316; 2006 White Paper, Korean Ministry of Defence, p. 7; Jae Ho Chung, *The Korean-American Alliance and the "Rise of China": A Preliminary Assessment of Perceptual Changes and Strategic Choices* (Stanford, CA: Stanford University, February 1999).

105 Bernett, *A Brief Analysis of the ROK's Defence Reform Plan*; Sheen, 'Out of

America, Into the Dragon's Arms', pp. 154–157; White Paper 2006, Korean Ministry of Defence, p. 29.

106 Interview with expert at the Korean National University, Seoul, 14 October 2007.

107 Interview with Vietnamese scholar, Singapore, 5 April 2010.

108 Stephen Walt, 'Alliance Formation and the Balance of World Power', *International Security*, vol. 9, no. 4, 1985, pp. 3–43; Jervis, 'Cooperation Under the Security Dilemma', pp. 167–214.

109 Peter Katzenstein, *The Culture of National Security* (New York: Columbia University Press, 1996), pp. 15–30.

Chapter Four

1 Interviews with defence officer, Delhi, 3 November 2008.

2 'Australia and India Sign Defence Information Sharing Agreement', *Defence and Security News*, 13 July 2007.

3 Jyotsna Bakshi, 'India–Russia Defence Co-operation', *Strategic Analysis*, vol. 30, no. 3, 2006, pp. 449–66.

4 'Japan, U.S. Poised to Keep Tokyo's Base-hosting Costs at Current Size', *Japan Today*, 24 October 2010.

5 William Overholt, *Asia, America, and the Transformation of Geopolitics*, (Cambridge: Cambridge University Press, 2009), p. 279.

6 Japan–Australia Joint Declaration on Security Cooperation, 13 March 2007, www.mofa.go.jp/region/asia-paci/australia/joint0703.html.

7 'Japan Keen on Boosting Security Ties with S Korea', *Japan Today*, 8 November 2010.

8 William Tow, 'ANZUS: Regional versus Global Security in Asia?' *International Relations of the Asia-Pacific*, vol. 5, no. 2, 2005, pp. 197–216. .

9 Andrew Forrest, 'How to be a Good Friend: China Considers Australia's East Asian Security Contributions in the Post-Howard Era?', *Security Challenges*, vol. 4, no. 1, 2008, pp. 43–53; Hugh White, 'The Limits of Optimism; Australia and the Rise of China', *Australian Journal of International Affairs*, vol. 59, no 4, 2008, p. 470.

10 Australian Department of Defence, *Defending Australia in the Asia Pacific Century: Force 2030* (Canberra: Department of Defence, 2009), p. 48.

11 'S. Korea, China Agree to Cooperate for Peace on Korean Peninsula', *Korea Times*, 29 May 2008.

12 Bim Yon-se, '34 Percent of Army Cadets Regard US as Main Enemy', *Korea Times*, 4 June 2008.

13 Don Oberdorfer, 'The United States and South Korea: Can This Alliance Last?' *Policy Forum,* 17 November 2007; Scott Snyder, 'The Beginning of the End of the US–ROK Alliance,' *PACNET,* 26 August 2004; Carin Zissis, 'The Fragile US–South Korean Alliance,' Council on Foreign Relations, 14 September 2006.

14 Snyder, 'The Future of US–ROK Relations', *Asian Perspective,* vol. 33, no. 2, 2008, p. 93–111.

15 Jonathan Holslag, 'Embracing China's Global Security Ambitions', *Washington Quarterly,* vol. 32, no. 3, pp. 105–18.

16 'Youxiao Yingdui Gezhong Chuantong He Fei Chuantong Anquan Weixie', Xinhua, 13 December 2006.

17 Quoted in Liu Congliang, 'Duoyuanhua Weixie Yaoqiu Zhongguo Junren Shuli Xin Guojia Anquan Guan', *Jiefangjun bao,* 15 July 2008.

18 'For China, Stability Inside and Outside Key for Future Prosperity', *Asahi Shimbun,* 12 June 2010.

19 Zhang Yan, interview with Zhang Xiaodong, 'Jie Du A Fu Han Da Xuan: Zhong Guo Xi Bu An Quan Li Yi Bu Shou Ying Xiang', *China Daily,* 20 August 2009.

20 Nan Zhimo, 'A Fu Han Wen Ti, Zhong Guo Ke Yi Geng Zhu Dong', *Nanfang Daily,* 1 April 2009.

21 Zhang, 'Jie Du A Fu Han Da Xuan: Zhong Guo Xi Bu An Quan Li Yi Bu Shou Ying Xiang'. See also 'Zhong Guo Jiang Chu Guo Fan Cong, Jie Fang Jun Hui Qu A Fu Han Ma?', www.cnjunshi.com, 5 August 2009; For an interesting interview with the Chinese Ambassador in Afghanistan on the protection of Chinese workers, see Li Shaofeng, 'A Fu Han Jing Cha Bao Hu Zhong Guo Gong Ren, Feng Xian Bu Xiao Shang Ji Bu Shao', *China Youth Daily,* 18 July 2004.

22 'China Mulling Naval Base in Gulf of Aden', *Global Times,* 31 November 2009.

23 Presentation by Zheng Hong at a conference on emerging Naval Powers, Norwegian Institute for Defence Studies, Oslo, 24–25 June 2010.

24 Jonathan Holslag, The New Security Frontier, *Strategic Analysis,* vol. 33, no. 5, 2009, pp. 652–63.

25 China invites military officers for training in China, has reportedly provided uniforms and telecommunications equipment and has more frequent dialogues between medium-level military cadres.

26 'E Luo Si Yi Yu Gong Gu Qi Zhan Lue Hou Fang', *People's Daily,* 4 August 2009. See also, 'E Luo Si Jiang Zai Ji Er Ji Si Si Tan Jian Li Di Er Ge Jun Shi Ji Di', Xinhua, 2 August 2009.

27 Song Xing, 'Shi Li Zhong Xin De Dong Tai Zhuan Yi Yu Zhong Ya Di Yuan Zheng', *Contemporary International Relations,* December 2004; Wu Fei, 'Zhong Guo Zai Zhong Ya De Zhan Lue Li Yi,' *Shang Chang Xian Dai Hua,* May 2005; Yin Zhaohui, 'Lun Zhong Guo Zai Zhong Ya De Di Yuan Li Yi, An Quan Kun Jing Yu Zhan Lue Xuan Ze', *Li Lun Dao Kan,* June 2007; Yang Luhui, 'Di Yuan Zheng Zhi Yan Bian Yu Zhong Guo Xin An Quan Guan- Yi Shanghai He Zuo Zu Zhi Xin Ji Zhi Wei Shi Jiao', *She Hui Ke Xue,* March 2007.

28 Yang Yun, 'Hou Mei Guo Zai Zhong Ya De Kuo Zhang Ji Qi Dui Zhong Guo Xi Bu Zhou Bian An Quan Huan Jing De Ying Xiang', *He Ping Yu Fa Zhan,* March 2006, pp. 50–4.

29 Xing Guancheng, 'Zhong Ya An Quan Yu An Quan He Zuo', *Dang Dai Shi Jie,* May 2006.

30 Yang Yun, 'Hou Mei Guo Zai Zhong Ya De Kuo Zhang Ji Qi Dui Zhong Guo Xi Bu Zhou Bian An Quan Huan Jing

De Ying Xiang'; Wang Xiaomei, 'Zhong Ya Shi You He Zuo Yu An Quan Zhan Lue', *Guo Ji Jing Ji He Zuo*, December 2006, pp. 16–21.

[31] Holslag, 'The New Security Frontier'.

[32] Chen Zhimi, 'Nationalism, Internationalism and Chinese Policy', *Journal of Contemporary China*, vol. 14, no. 1, 2006, p. 47; Christopher Hughes, *Chinese Nationalism in the Global Era* (London and New York: Routledge, 2006).

[33] The following studies look closer into the issue of nationalism in China, India and Japan's foreign policies: Susan Shirk, *China: Fragile Superpower*, (Oxford: Oxford University Press, 2007); Hughes, *Chinese Nationalism in the Global Era*; Hughes, 'Nationalism and Multilateralism in Chinese Foreign Policy: Implications for Southeast Asia', *Pacific Review*, vol. 18, no. 1, 2005, pp. 119–35; Pyle, *Japan Rising: The Resurgence of Japanese Power and Purpose* (New York: Public Affairs, 2008); Stephen Cohen, *India: Emerging Power* (Washington DC: Brookings Institution Press, 2008), pp. 110–16.

Conclusion

[1] Joseph Hewitt, Jonathan Wilkenfeld and Ted Robert Gurr, *Peace and Conflict 2010* (Baltimore, MD: Center for International Development and Conflict Management, 2010), pp. 8–16; Daniel Kauffmann, Aart Kraay and Massimo Mastruzzy, 'Governance Matters VIII: Aggregate and Individual Governance Indicators', *World Bank Policy Research Working Paper*, no. 4978 (Washington DC, World Bank, 2009).

[2] Hewitt et al., *Peace and Conflict 2010*, pp. 11–16; Robert Rotberg, 'State Failure and States Poised to Fail: Asia and Developing Nations', *Ilmin Forum for International Affairs and Security Policy Brief*, no. 5, 18 December 2009. See also, Rotberg (ed.), *When States Fail: Causes and Consequences* (Princeton, NJ: Princeton University Press, 2004).

[3] David Wivell, 'China Slams US For Selling Arms To Taiwan', AP and *Huffington Post*, 20 August 2009.

Adelphi books are published eight times a year by Routledge Journals, an imprint of Taylor & Francis, 4 Park Square, Milton Park, Abingdon, Oxfordshire OX14 4RN, UK.

A subscription to the institution print edition, ISSN 0567-932X, includes free access for any number of concurrent users across a local area network to the online edition, ISSN 1478-5145.

2011 Annual Adelphi Subscription Rates			
Institution	£491	$864 USD	€726
Individual	£230	$391 USD	€312
Online only	£442	$778 USD	€653

Dollar rates apply to subscribers outside Europe. Euro rates apply to all subscribers in Europe except the UK and the Republic of Ireland where the pound sterling price applies. All subscriptions are payable in advance and all rates include postage. Journals are sent by air to the USA, Canada, Mexico, India, Japan and Australasia. Subscriptions are entered on an annual basis, i.e. January to December. Payment may be made by sterling cheque, dollar cheque, international money order, National Giro, or credit card (Amex, Visa, Mastercard).

For more information, visit our website: **http://www.informaworld.com/ adelphipapers.**

For a complete and up-to-date guide to Taylor & Francis journals and books publishing programmes, and details of advertising in our journals, visit our website: **http://www.informaworld.com.**

Ordering information:
USA/Canada: Taylor & Francis Inc., Journals Department, 325 Chestnut Street, 8th Floor, Philadelphia, PA 19106, USA. **UK/Europe/Rest of World:** Routledge Journals, T&F Customer Services, T&F Informa UK Ltd., Sheepen Place, Colchester, Essex, CO3 3LP, UK.

Advertising enquiries to:
USA/Canada: The Advertising Manager, Taylor & Francis Inc., 325 Chestnut Street, 8th Floor, Philadelphia, PA 19106, USA. Tel: +1 (800) 354 1420. Fax: +1 (215) 625 2940.

UK/Europe/Rest of World: The Advertising Manager, Routledge Journals, Taylor & Francis, 4 Park Square, Milton Park, Abingdon, Oxfordshire OX14 4RN, UK. Tel: +44 (0) 20 7017 6000. Fax: +44 (0) 20 7017 6336.

The print edition of this journal is printed on ANSI conforming acid-free paper by Bell & Bain, Glasgow, UK.

1944-5571(2010)50:5;1-F